# impact

# Foundation

| | <br>**1**<br>**Family Matters**<br>page 26 | <br>**2**<br>**A Different Education**<br>page 42 | 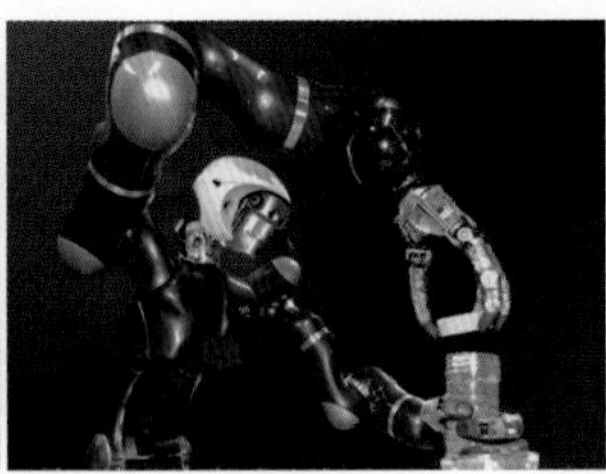<br>**3**<br>**Robots and Us**<br>page 60 | <br>**4**<br>**Part of Nature**<br>page 76 |
|---|---|---|---|---|
| THEME | Family and traditions | Schools around the world | People interacting with technology | People and animals and their place in nature |
| VOCABULARY STRATEGY | Adjective + dependent preposition | Antonyms | The *-able* ending | Compound words |
| SPEAKING STRATEGY | Asking and answering personal questions | Talking about likes and dislikes | Reacting | Checking facts |
| GRAMMAR | ***Be* and *have got*:**<br>*I'm friendly, but my sister isn't.*<br>**Countable and uncountable nouns:**<br>*Are there any biscuits in the cupboard? Yes, there are.*<br>*Is there any water in the bottle? Yes, there is.* | **Present simple:** Talking about routines, habits and permanent states<br>*She doesn't have lunch at school. She goes home for lunch.*<br>**Adverbs of frequency:** Saying how often you do something<br>*I rarely forget to do my homework.* | ***Can* and *can't*:** Talking about ability<br>*My robot can talk, but it can't open doors.*<br>***Should* and *shouldn't*:** Giving advice<br>*They should study for this maths test.*<br>*You shouldn't buy this robot. It's very expensive.* | **Quantifiers:** Talking and asking about quantity<br>*How many different kinds of camels are there? There are two kinds of camels.*<br>**Adverbs:** Saying how you do something<br>*Elephants can swim very well.*<br>*The three-toed sloth moves very slowly.* |
| READING | *Breakfast in Four Countries* | *Growth Mindset* | *Girls Can Code* | *A Wild Animal Isn't a Pet* |
| READING STRATEGY | Make predictions based on visuals | Identify the main idea | Identify the main point of a paragraph | Identify sequence of events |
| VIDEO | *Celebrating the Dead* | *Education Around the World* | *Squishy Robot Fingers* | *Into the Real Wild: Photographing Pandas with Ami Vitale* |
| MISSION | **Discover Your Values**<br>National Geographic Explorer: **Max Lowe**, Photographer/ Writer | **Believe in Yourself**<br>National Geographic Explorers: **Dave and Amy Freeman**, Adventurers/ Educators | **Change the World**<br>National Geographic Explorer: **Chad Jenkins**, Computer Scientist/ Roboticist | **Use Your Skills**<br>National Geographic Explorer: **Juliana Machado Ferreira**, Conservation Biologist |
| WRITING | Genre: **Personal description**<br>Focus: Connect and contrast | Genre: **Sequencing paragraph**<br>Focus: Use sequencing words | Genre: **Contrast paragraph**<br>Focus: Use contrast words | Genre: **Fact sheet**<br>Focus: Categorise and label information |
| PRONUNCIATION | Syllables and stress | The third person -s and -es endings | The *th* sound | Short vowel sounds |
| EXPRESS YOURSELF | Creative Expression: **Text messages**<br>*World Food Day*<br>Making connections: Family, food and school | | Creative Expression: **Advertisement**<br>*Robotosaurus Rex*<br>Making connections: Robots and animals | |

| | **5** **Water** page 94 | **6** **The City: Past, Present and Future** page 110 | **7** **Amazing Space** page 128 | **8** **See the World** page 144 |
|---|---|---|---|---|
| THEME | How to protect and preserve water | Architecture, photography and preservation of cities | Space and technology | Travel and holidays |
| VOCABULARY STRATEGY | Prefix *un-* | Collocations with *take* | Upper vs. lower case | Suffix *-ist* |
| SPEAKING STRATEGY | Brainstorming solutions | Expressing opinions and responding to them | Making and responding to suggestions | Asking for and giving directions |
| GRAMMAR | **Present continuous:** Talking about what is happening now and about things that always happen<br>*My brother is always having long showers!*<br>***There was* and *There were*:** Talking about the past<br>*There were a lot of dead fish in the river.* | **Past simple:** Talking about the past<br>*They took photos of a temple, a church and a castle there.*<br>**Past simple:** Asking questions about the past<br>*Where did you go last summer?*<br>*We went to Beijing. We didn't fly there. We went by train.* | **Comparatives:** Comparing two things<br>*Saturn is much bigger than Earth, but it's smaller than Jupiter.*<br>**Superlatives:** Comparing three or more things<br>*Jupiter is bigger than Saturn, but the biggest object in our solar system is the sun.* | ***Going to*:** Describing future plans<br>*What are you going to do for your birthday?*<br>***In*, *on* and *at*:** Saying when things happen<br>*On Friday, we're going to fly to Prague.* |
| READING | *An Ocean of Plastic* | *Queen of the Curve* | *Satellites Above* | *Kite-skiing in the Arctic* |
| READING STRATEGY | Look for examples and explanations | Identify author's purpose | Connect text to prior knowledge | Visualise |
| VIDEO | *Boyan's Big Idea* | *Preserving Our Heritage with Ross Davison* | *The Electric Wind of Venus* | *Student Expedition: Tanzania* |
| MISSION | **Protect Our Water**<br>National Geographic Explorer: **Osvel Hinojosa Huerta**, Conservationist | **Know Your History**<br>National Geographic Explorer: **Ross Davison**, Heritage Conservationist | **Think Like a Scientist**<br>National Geographic Explorer: **Brendan Mullan**, Astrobiologist | **Get Outside!**<br>National Geographic Explorer: **Sarah McNair-Landry**, Adventurer/Cinematographer |
| WRITING | Genre: **Persuasive paragraph**<br>Focus: Use persuasive phrases to give advice | Genre: **Paragraph of opinion**<br>Focus: Give reasons to support your opinion | Genre: **Compare and contrast paragraph**<br>Focus: Use words for comparison and contrast | Genre: **Blog post**<br>Focus: Identify and include parts of a blog |
| PRONUNCIATION | Long vowel sounds | The *n* and *ng* sounds | The soft and hard *g* sounds | Silent letters |
| EXPRESS YOURSELF | Creative Expression: **Tour description**<br>*A Tour of Thun, Switzerland*<br>Making connections: Water, buildings and history | | Creative Expression: **Blog**<br>*Welcome to Haneul's Awesome Blogging World*<br>Making connections: Space and travel | |

# Meet the Explorers

## Unit 1

MAX LOWE **Photographer/Writer**

A sense of adventure runs in Max Lowe's family. Max's father, Alex, died in a climbing accident when Max was young. Max's father inspired him. Now, Max travels with his step-father, Conrad, who is also a climber. Max writes about their adventures and takes photos to remember their experiences together.

## Unit 2

DAVE AND AMY FREEMAN **Adventurers/Educators**

Dave and Amy Freeman were named National Geographic Adventurers of the Year in 2014. They are husband and wife. They explore by foot, kayak, canoe and even dogsled! The Freemans also record their adventures for thousands of students to watch all over the world. Their video lessons inspire students to explore.

## Unit 3

CHAD JENKINS **Computer Scientist/Roboticist**

Chad Jenkins builds robots. He teaches his robots to do things, but he doesn't do it alone. He asks people to visit his online lab. People give Chad ideas for new things they would like to see his robots do. Chad's robots can help out around the house, or even play sports! What do you want to ask Chad's robots to do?

## Unit 4

JULIANA MACHADO FERREIRA **Conservation Biologist**

Juliana Machado Ferreira lives in Brazil, where some people take birds from their homes in the wild to sell them as pets. When she was a child, Juliana's parents taught her to love animals. Now, Juliana teaches others to love animals and to understand their role in nature. She also uses DNA information to return birds to their homes in the wild.

## Unit 5

OSVEL HINOJOSA HUERTA **Conservationist**

Where does your water come from? Osvel Hinojosa Huerta wants you to think about that. He wants to protect water. Osvel works in Mexico. There, the Colorado River doesn't flow like it used to. If the river dries out, wildlife will die with it. People who live near it will also suffer. But Osvel is hopeful. He's working with local people to make the wetlands wet again!

## Unit 6

ROSS DAVISON **Heritage Conservationist**

When Ross Davison finished college, he started working for an organisation called CyArk. There, he uses special cameras to preserve heritage sites around the world. He also works with the local people and students in each country to teach them how to use the equipment themselves. With Ross's help, we can save our history.

## Unit 7

BRENDAN MULLAN **Astrobiologist**

Brendan Mullan has loved space since he was a child. He especially likes studying how stars form in different galaxies. Brendan has worked as a teacher, a researcher and a science camp counsellor. Most recently, he co-founded *The Wrinkled Brain Project* to help students think about science, and design their own experiments.

## Unit 8

SARAH MCNAIR-LANDRY **Adventurer/Cinematographer**

Sarah NcNair-Landry skied to the South Pole when she was 18. She was the youngest person to do this. But she didn't stop there. She often travels by dogsled from her home in Alaska to go on other adventures. Sarah and her brother, Eric, once kite-skiied across Canada's Northwest Passage. It took them 85 days, and 200 chocolate bars!

Unit 0

# Welcome!

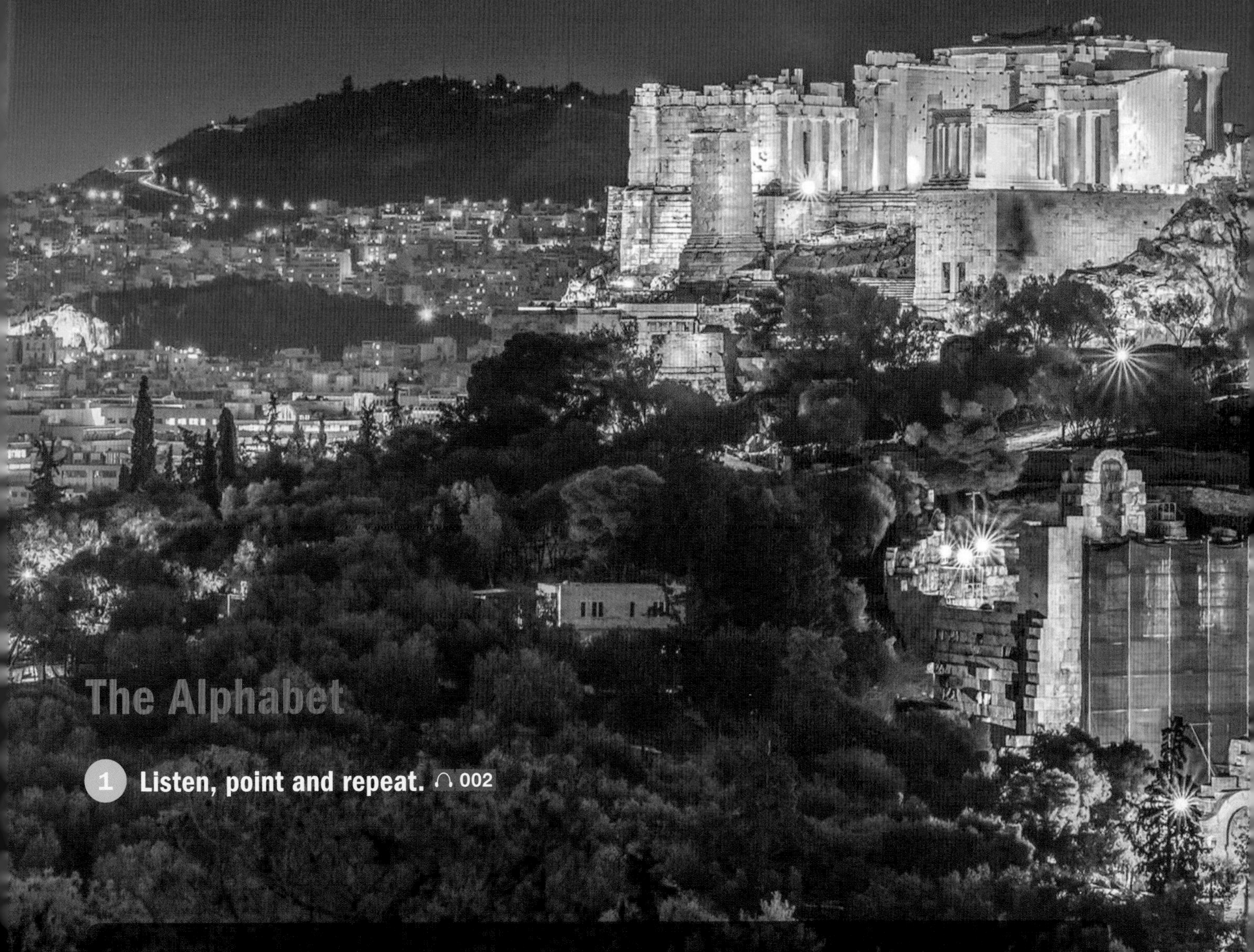

## The Alphabet

1 **Listen, point and repeat.** 002

Aa Bb Cc Dd Ee Ff Gg Hh Ii
Jj Kk Ll Mm Nn Oo Pp Qq Rr
Ss Tt Uu Vv Ww Xx Yy Zz

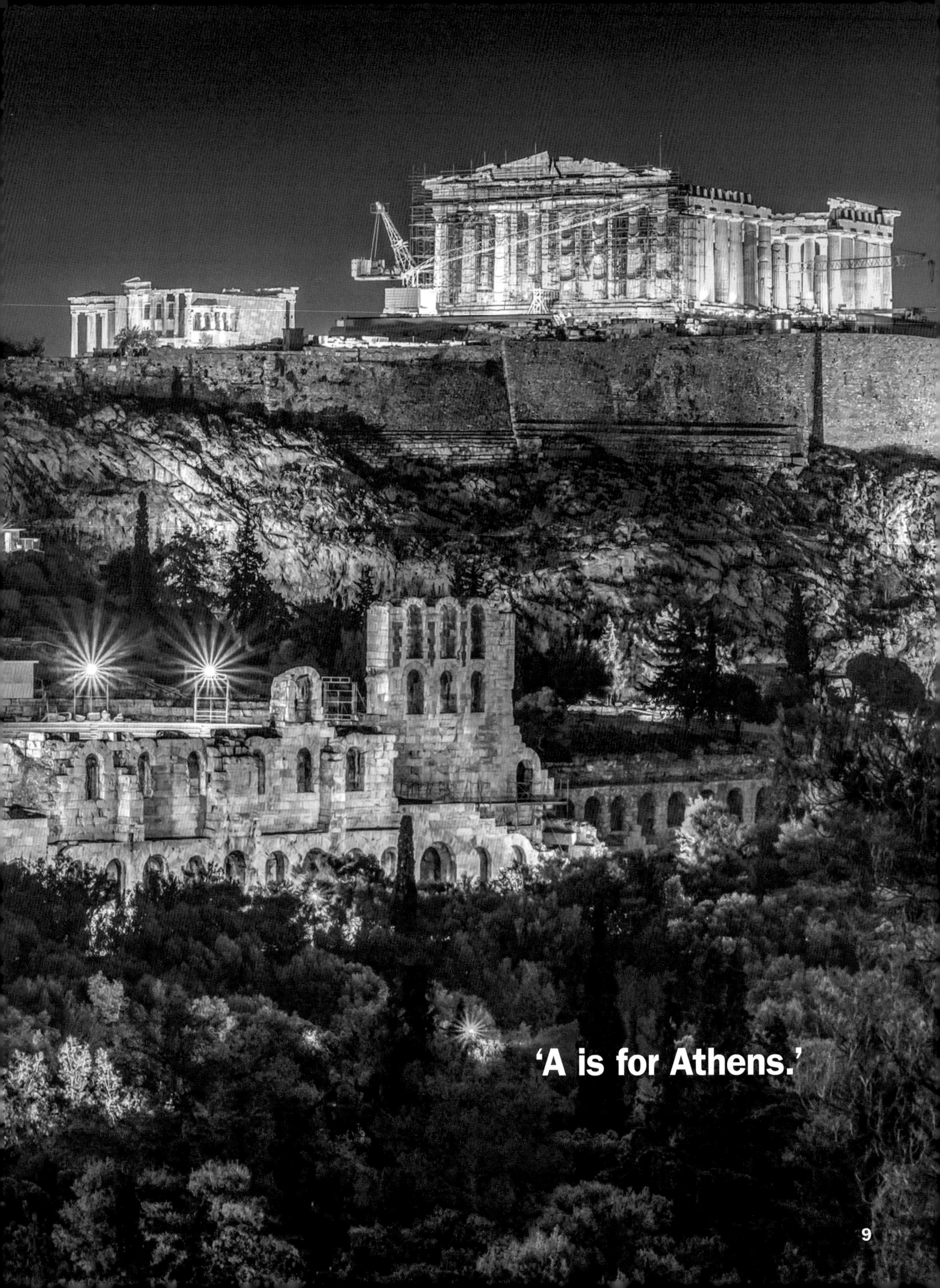
'A is for Athens.'

World map, Lisbon, Portugal

**1** **Listen and repeat.** 003

| Greetings and Introductions | | Questions |
|---|---|---|
| Hi! | Hello! | What's your name? |
| I'm Benjamina. | My name's Tarek. | Where are you from? |
| This is Julia. | Good / Nice to meet you. | |

**2** **Read and listen.** Underline the greetings and introductions. Circle the questions in blue. 004

Nadia: Hi! I'm Nadia. What's your name?
Chang: Hi, Nadia. My name's Chang. I'm from China.
Nadia: Good to meet you, Chang.
Chang: Where are you from?
Nadia: I'm from Turkey. This is my friend Gabriel. He's from Argentina.
Chang: Hello, Gabriel. Nice to meet you.
Gabriel: Hi! Nice to meet you, too!
Mrs Martin: OK! I think we're all ready to start. Welcome to your new English class! My name is Mrs Martin. I'm from Australia.

**3** **Complete the sentences with the words from the box.**

| **Argentinian** | **Chinese** | **Australian** | **Turkish** |
|---|---|---|---|

1. Nadia is ______________.
2. Chang is ______________.
3. Gabriel is ______________.
4. Mrs. Martin is ______________.

4 **Listen and repeat.** 005

## GRAMMAR

**Subject pronouns and *be***

| Full forms | Contractions | Full forms | Contractions |
|---|---|---|---|
| I am | I'm | I am not | I'm not |
| You are | You're | You are not | You aren't |
| He/She/It is | He's/She's/It's | He/She/It is not | He/She/It isn't |
| We are | We're | We are not | We aren't |
| You are | You're | You are not | You aren't |
| They are | They're | They are not | They aren't |

My name's Sara. I'm from Spain.
His name's Alan. He's from France. He isn't from Spain.

5 **Look at Activity 2 again.** Circle all the examples of the verb *be* in red.

6 **Listen and match.** Then make sentences. 006

| Brazil | Spain | Malaysia | Bulgaria | Mexico |
|---|---|---|---|---|

| Bulgarian | Spanish | Mexican | Brazilian | Malaysian |
|---|---|---|---|---|

1. Nor is Malaysian. She's from Malaysia.
2. Karina ______
3. Daniel ______
4. Andrei ______
5. Alicia and Sandra ______

7 **Work in groups.** Imagine you are in Australia for a month to study English. Copy and complete the card to the right. Ask and answer.

Hi, I'm Junko. What's your name?

Hi, Junko. My name's Mayumi.

**STUDENT REGISTRATION**
English Language School

Name: ______

Nationality: ______

## Classroom Language

**1** **Listen and repeat.** 007

# TEACHER

- **Sit down, please!**
- **Be quiet, please!**
- **Open your books at page 5.**
- **Listen to the recording.**
- **Work in pairs.**
- **Hurry up, please!**
- **Close the door, please.**
- **Write your answers in your books.**

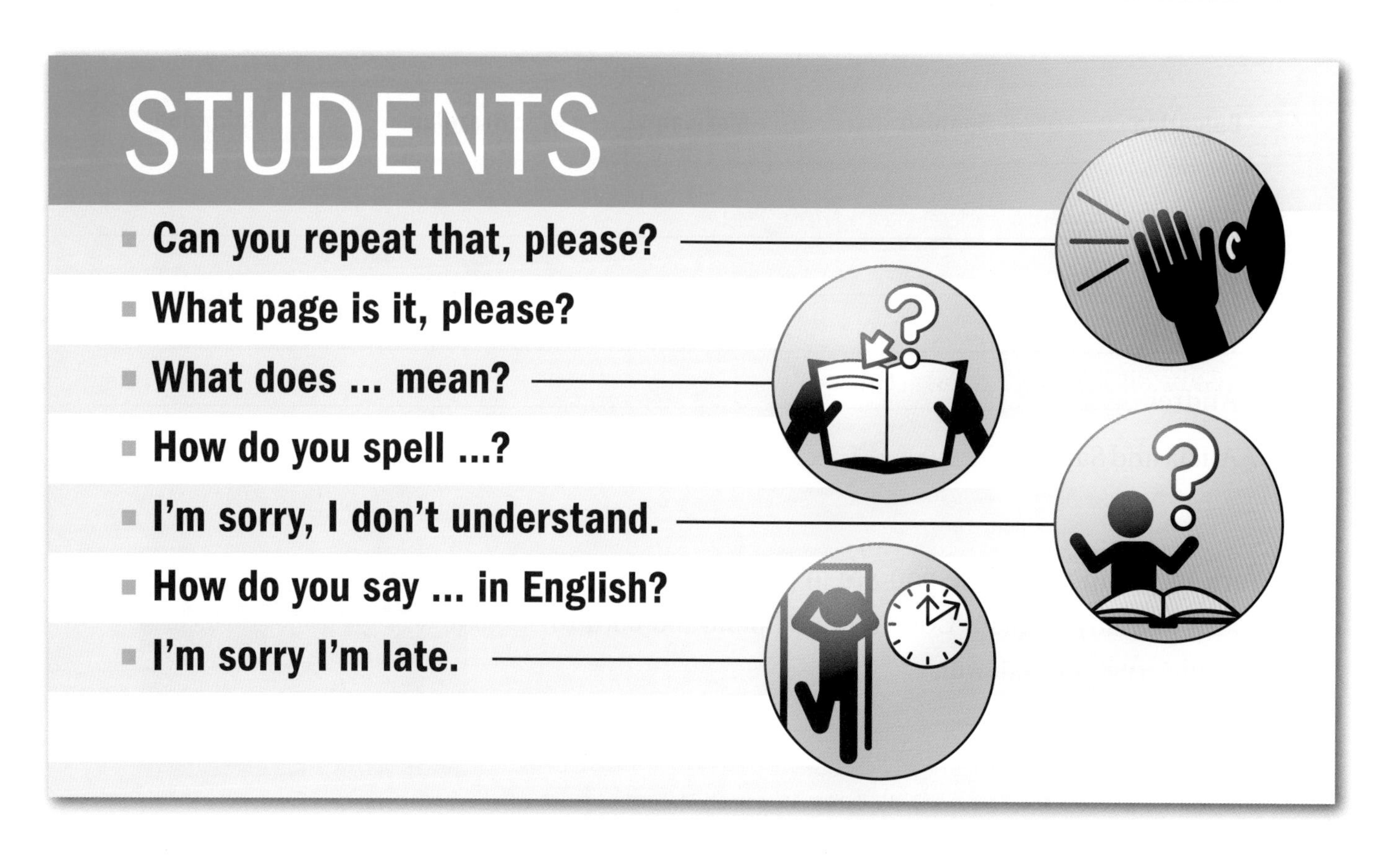

**2** **Read and listen.** 008

Mrs Martin: Be quiet, please! Open your books at page 40.

Daniel: Can you repeat that, please?

Mrs Martin: Open your books at page 40. Let's look at the photo. He's a National Geographic Explorer. What's his name?

Nadia: His name is Max Lowe.

Mrs Martin: Yes, that's right. Well done, Nadia. Now let's watch ...

Alberto: I'm sorry I'm late, Mrs Martin.

Mrs Martin: Hurry up, please, Alberto! Gabriel, don't talk to Chang.

Gabriel: Sorry, Mrs Martin.

Mrs Martin: Now, let's watch ...

Alicia: Mrs Martin, I can't see.

Mrs Martin: Oh. Well, move your chair over here. Good. Now. Is everyone ready? Let's watch the video.

**3** **Work in small groups.** Act out the conversation from Activity 2.

**4** **Now make up your own conversation.** Use classroom language from Activity 1.

# Months of the Year and Days of the Week

**1 Listen and repeat.** 009

| January | February | March | April |
|---|---|---|---|
| May | June | July | August |
| September | October | November | December |

**2 Listen and repeat.** 010

| Monday | Tuesday | Wednesday | Thursday | Friday | Saturday | Sunday |
|---|---|---|---|---|---|---|

**3 Work in pairs.** Ask and answer questions.

What day is it today?
It's Monday.

What month is it?
It's August.

# Seasons

**1 Listen and repeat.** 011

**2 Work in pairs.** Ask and answer questions.

What season is it?
It's summer.

What season is it?
It's the dry season.

## Numbers

**1** **Listen and repeat.** 012

| | | |
|---|---|---|
| 1 | one | first |
| 2 | two | second |
| 3 | three | third |
| 4 | four | fourth |
| 5 | five | fifth |
| 6 | six | sixth |
| 7 | seven | seventh |
| 8 | eight | eighth |
| 9 | nine | ninth |
| 10 | ten | tenth |
| 11 | eleven | eleventh |
| 12 | twelve | twelfth |
| 13 | thirteen | thirteenth |
| 14 | fourteen | fourteenth |
| 15 | fifteen | fifteenth |
| 16 | sixteen | sixteenth |
| 17 | seventeen | seventeenth |

| | | |
|---|---|---|
| 18 | eighteen | eighteenth |
| 19 | nineteen | nineteenth |
| 20 | twenty | twentieth |
| 21 | twenty-one | twenty-first |
| 22 | twenty-two | twenty-second |
| 30 | thirty | thirtieth |
| 40 | forty | fortieth |
| 50 | fifty | fiftieth |
| 60 | sixty | sixtieth |
| 70 | seventy | seventieth |
| 80 | eighty | eightieth |
| 90 | ninety | ninetieth |
| 100 | one hundred | hundredth |
| 101 | one hundred and one | |
| 235 | two hundred and thirty-five | |
| 999 | nine hundred and ninety-nine | |
| 1000 | one thousand | |

**2** **Work in groups.** Ask and answer questions.

# Colours

1 Listen and repeat. 013

2 Point and say.

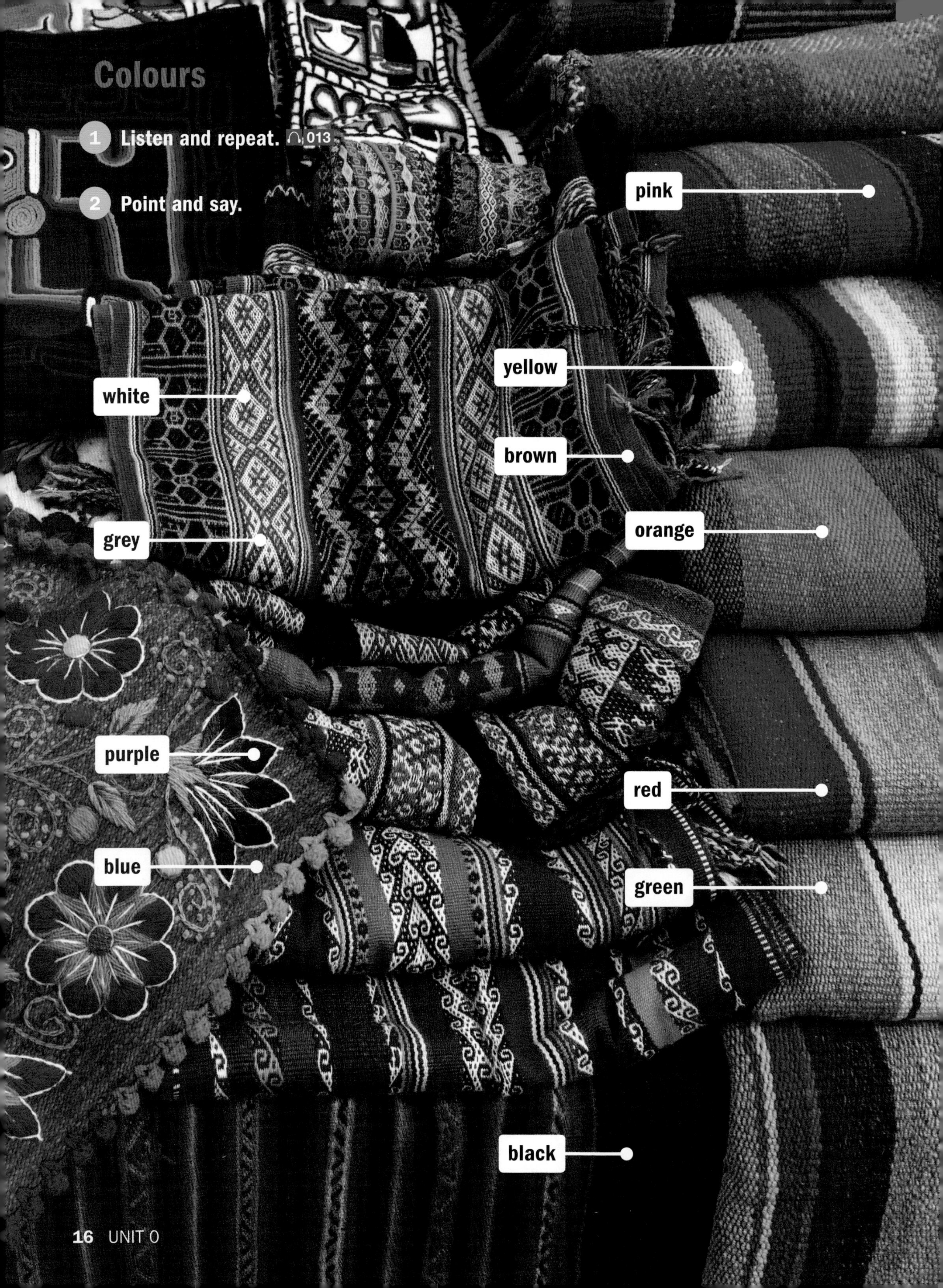

# Telling the Time

**1 Listen and repeat.** 014

**The Time** What time is it?

| It's one o'clock. | It's half past two. It's two thirty. | It's quarter to three. It's two forty-five. | It's quarter past four. It's four fifteen. |
|---|---|---|---|

in the morning | in the afternoon | in the evening

**2 Work in pairs.** Look at the map of Australia. Write the times in words. Then read.



What time is it in Perth?
It's three o'clock in the afternoon.

What time is it in Darwin?
It's ______________________.

What time is it in Cairns?
It's ______________________.

What time is it in Sydney?
It's ______________________.

What time is it in Adelaide?
It's ______________________.

**3 Work in pairs.** Ask and answer.

Lunch is at one o'clock.

**What time is ...**

- lunch?
- breakfast?
- your favourite club?
- your first lesson at school
- your favourite TV programme?
- your last lesson at school?

## 1 Listen and repeat. 015

### GRAMMAR

**Object pronouns**

| | |
|---|---|
| It's for **me**. | I don't like **it**. |
| This is for **you**. | Come with **us**. |
| It belongs to **him**. | It belongs to **you**. |
| I'm with **her**. | It's for **them**. |

## 2 Listen and read. Circle the object pronouns. 016

1. Maria: Hi, Francesco. Where's Teresa?
   Francesco: I don't know. She isn't at school today.
   Maria: Oh, I usually have lunch with her.

2. Stefano: I like your bike. It's really cool!
   Anna: Thank you! I love it.

3. Roberto: Who's that boy?
   Claudia: I don't know him. He's a new student here.

4. Antonio: Hurry up, Luca! It's half past three. We're late!
   Luca: I know! Mrs Martin is angry with us again!

## 3 Circle the correct words.

1. Who is this girl? *I / Me* don't know *she / her*.
2. *He / Him* is a very good student.
3. Where is my book? *I / Us* can't find *him / it*.
4. *Us / We* are in classroom B today.
5. *He / Him* doesn't like *we / us*.
6. Look at the shoes! I like *they / them*.

**1** **Listen and repeat.** 017

## GRAMMAR

**Possessive adjectives**

| | |
|---|---|
| It's **my** cat. | This is **its** food. |
| Is this **your** house? | Are these **your** books? |
| No, it's **his** house. | Yes, they're **our** books. |
| It's **her** bag. | Where are **their** books? |

**2** **Circle the correct word.**

1. Carla's got a twin brother. *His* / *Her* name is Pedro.
2. They've got one cat. *Its* / *Their* name is Cosmo.
3. Carla and Pedro like purple. It's *his* / *their* favourite colour.
4. I love purple, too. It's *my* / *her* favourite colour!

**3** **Look at the photo.** Complete the sentences with the names. Circle the correct word.

1. ____________ likes hiking with *her* / *their* dad.
2. ____________ 's top is blue. *His* / *Her* rucksack is red and black.
3. ____________ 's shorts are grey. *His* / *Our* rucksack is green.
4. ____________ 's hair is grey. ____________ 's hair is a different colour. *Her* / *Our* hair is brown.
5. ____________ and ____________ like the flowers in the mountains. *Their* / *Its* favourite flowers are yellow.

## 1 Listen and repeat. 018

### GRAMMAR

**Possessive pronouns**

This is my book. This book is **mine**.
This is your phone. This phone is **yours**.
This is his bike. This bike is **his**.
This is her bag. This bag is **hers**.
This is your house. This house is **yours**.

This is our school. This school is **ours**.
These are their shoes. These shoes are **theirs**.

**Question word: Whose?**
**Whose** house is this?
It's **mine.**

## 2 Listen and read. Circle the correct word. Then listen and check. 019

Penny: Is this your book, Ana?

Ana: No, it isn't *my / mine* . Is it *your / yours* ?

Penny: No, it isn't. There's Sara! Maybe it's *her / hers* .
Sara, is this book *your / yours* ?

Sara: Yes, it is. It's *my / mine* !
Thank you!

## 3 Complete the conversation with the words from the box.

Mrs Martin: Adam, where is ______________ book?

Adam: I'm sorry, Mrs Martin. It isn't in ______________ bag. I don't know where it is.

Mrs Martin: Jan, there are two books on your desk. Are they ______________ ?

Jan: Yes, they are ______________ , Mrs Martin. This is ______________ English book, and this is ______________ maths book.

## 4 Write.

| her | hers | mine | yours | whose |
|---|---|---|---|---|

Khaled: ______________ kite is this? Is it ______________ , Zain?

Zain: It isn't ______________ . Is it ______________ ?

Khaled: Yes. Look, ______________ name is on it.

## Plurals

**1 Listen and repeat.** 020

| singular | plural | singular | plural |
|---|---|---|---|
| girl | girl**s** | bus | bus**es** |
| boy | boy**s** | watch | watch**es** |
| teacher | teacher**s** | box | box**es** |
| | | quiz | quiz**zes** |
| **singular** | **plural** | potato | potato**es** |
| baby | bab**ies** | class | class**es** |
| country | countr**ies** | | |

| singular | plural |
|---|---|
| child | children |
| woman | women |
| man | men |
| person | people |
| mouse | mice |
| deer | deer |
| sheep | sheep |
| tooth | teeth |
| foot | feet |

**2 Work in pairs.** Take turns. Use a coin to move. (Heads = 1 space; tails = 2 spaces) Is the word plural? Say the singular. Is the word singular? Say the plural.

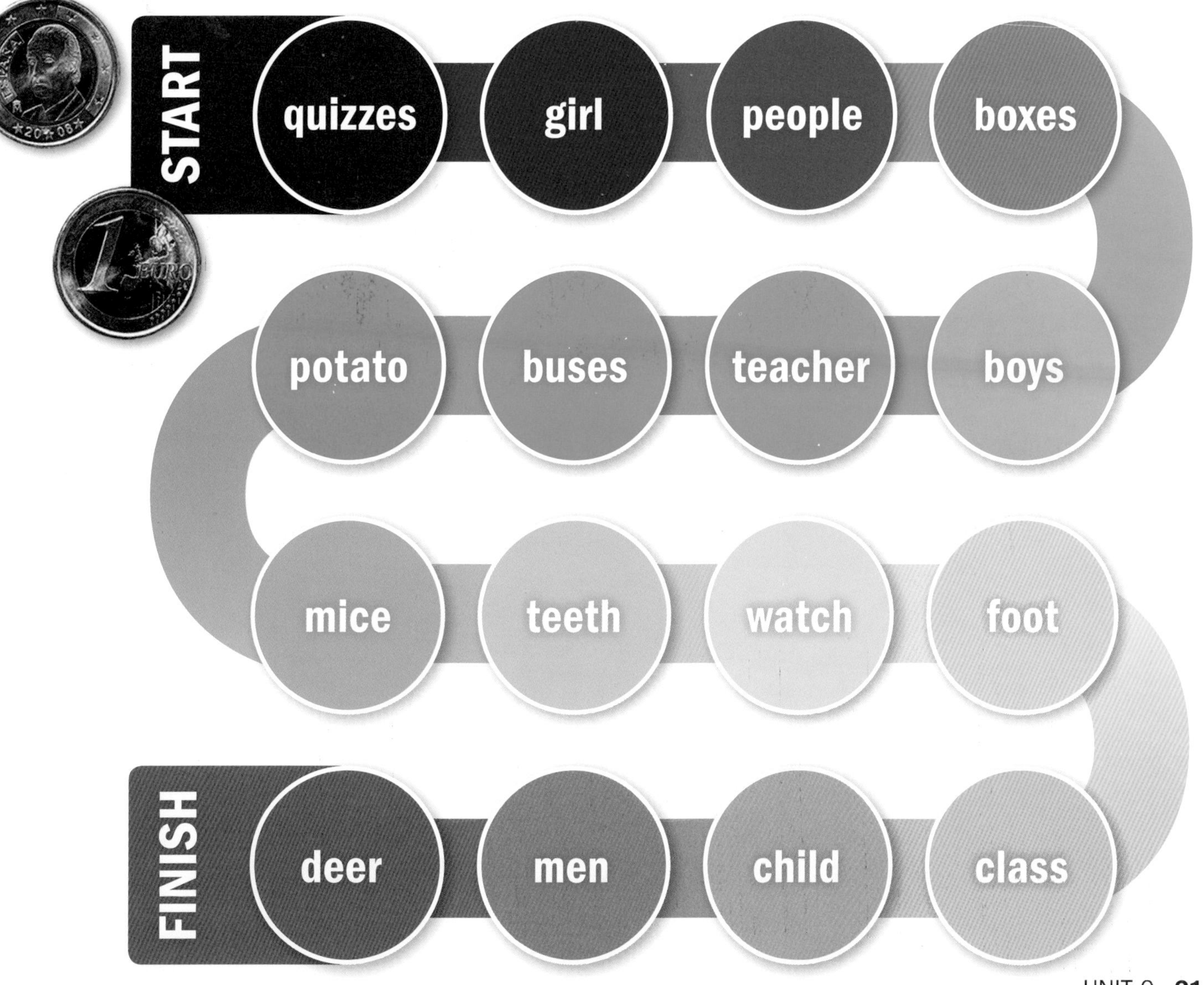

## 1 Listen and repeat. 021

GRAMMAR

**Definite and indefinite articles**

There is **a** book in my bag. **The** book is red.
There is **an** apple on the table. **The** apple is green.
Who are **the** students in your classroom?

## 2 Complete the sentences with *a*, *an* or *the*.

1. Alberto is __________ student at my school.
2. There's __________ umbrella in my bag.
3. __________ books on this desk are mine.
4. I've got __________ new bike. __________ bike is purple.
5. A: Where is __________ English teacher?
   B: He's in __________ school office.

1 **Listen and repeat.** 022

GRAMMAR

**Demonstrative adjectives**

**This** flower is pink.

She wants **that** flower.

**These** flowers are pretty.

I like **those** orange flowers.

2 **Read the sentences.** Are the underlined words singular or plural, near or far? Tick two boxes for each sentence.

| | Singular | Plural | Near | Far |
|---|---|---|---|---|
| 1. This bike is red. | ☑ | ☐ | ☑ | ☐ |
| 2. Is that your house? | ☐ | ☐ | ☐ | ☐ |
| 3. These umbrellas are purple. | ☐ | ☐ | ☐ | ☐ |
| 4. That cat is black. | ☐ | ☐ | ☐ | ☐ |
| 5. Are those shoes new? | ☐ | ☐ | ☐ | ☐ |
| 6. She wants to read this book. | ☐ | ☐ | ☐ | ☐ |
| 7. Who is that girl? | ☐ | ☐ | ☐ | ☐ |
| 8. That phone is cool! | ☐ | ☐ | ☐ | ☐ |

3 **Work in pairs.** Describe things in the classroom. Use *this*, *that*, *these* and *those* to talk about them.

This bag is big.

Those pencils are yellow.

**1 Listen and repeat.** Where is the cat? 023

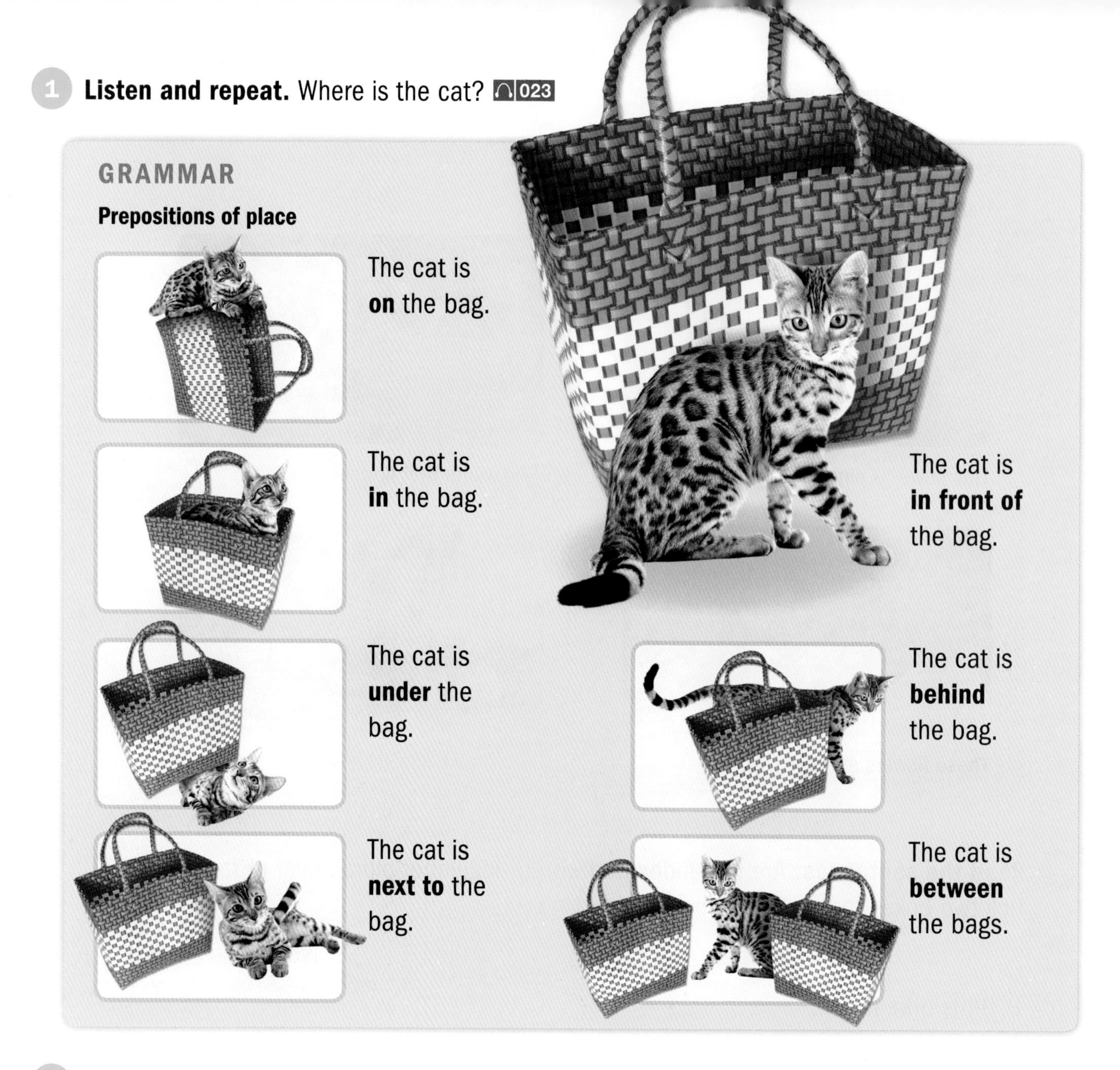

**GRAMMAR**

**Prepositions of place**

The cat is **on** the bag.

The cat is **in** the bag.

The cat is **under** the bag.

The cat is **next to** the bag.

The cat is **in front of** the bag.

The cat is **behind** the bag.

The cat is **between** the bags.

**2 Work in pairs.** Look at the pictures in Activity 1.

- Choose a picture.
- Describe where the cat is.
- Can your partner point to the correct picture?

**3 Draw a simple picture.** Don't show it to your partner. Include these things.

| | | | |
|---|---|---|---|
| **a table** | **a chair** | **an animal** | **a box** |
| **a hat** | **some books** | **some pencils** | **a banana** |

- Describe your picture to your partner.
- Use prepositions of place.
- Can your partner draw your picture?

There's a chair next to a table.
There are some books under the chair.
There's a box on the chair.

## 1 Listen and repeat. 024

### GRAMMAR

**Countable and uncountable nouns**

| Countable nouns | Uncountable nouns |
|---|---|
| There's **an apple** on the table. | There's **some juice** on the table. |
| There are **some apples** in the fridge. | There's **some bread** on the table. |

## 2 Complete the sentences with *a*, *an* or *some*.

1. There is ___some___ juice and ________ bread.
2. There is ________ egg.
3. There are ________ tomatoes and ________ strawberries.
4. There is ________ cheese.

## 3 Talk about the food in your fridge at home.

There is some butter.

There are some tomatoes.

Unit 1

# Family Matters

Explorers Max Lowe and Conrad Anker

'My dad was superhuman to me.'
**Max Lowe**

### TO START

1. Look at the photo. Guess. How are the people related?
2. What does 'superhuman' mean to you?
3. Who are your heroes? Are they famous people, friends or people in your family?

**1** **Do you know any famous families?**
Discuss. Then listen and read. 025

## The Cousteau Family

Jacques Cousteau was a great marine explorer. Many people enjoy his books and films about the sea. His **son**, Philippe Sr, also loved the sea and made films about it. Now his **grandson**, Philippe Jr, and his **granddaughter**, Alexandra, want to protect the sea. 'My father and grandfather were an inspiration,' says Alexandra.

Meave and Louise Leakey working together, Kenya

## The Lowe-Anker Family

Conrad Anker **is married to** Jennifer Lowe-Anker. Jennifer's first **husband**, Alex Lowe, was a very famous climber. He **died** in a climbing accident in 1999. Alex and Conrad were very close friends and Conrad is also very good at climbing. In fact, he's also a professional climber. When Alex died, Conrad helped to **take care of** Jennifer's **children**, Max, Isaac and Sam. Max now works with his **step-father**. 'Conrad is my hero and my mentor,' he says.

## The Leakey Family

Palaeoanthropologists are scientists who are interested in fossils and early human life. There are three **generations** of palaeoanthropologists in the Leakey family. Mary and Louis Leakey were very famous for their important work in the 1940s and 50s. Their son, Richard Leakey, is also interested in early human life. Richard and his **wife**, Meave, have got two **daughters**, Louise and Samira. Meave and Louise now work together.

**2** **LEARN NEW WORDS Listen and repeat.** 026

**3** **Work in pairs.** Name one of your heroes. What do you know about his or her family? Take notes. Compare your notes with your partner's.

## 4 Read and write the words from the list.

| child | daughter | died | husband | is married to | son | step-father | wife |
|---|---|---|---|---|---|---|---|

Max Lowe is a National Geographic photographer and writer. He travels around the world and takes photos of amazing places. He is the ______________ of Jennifer Lowe-Anker and Alex Lowe. Alex was Jennifer's first ______________. He ______________ in a climbing accident in 1999, when Max was a young ______________. Now, Jennifer ______________ another famous climber, Conrad Anker. Conrad is Max's ______________. Max and Conrad enjoy climbing and travelling together.

## 5 LEARN NEW WORDS Listen to these words and match them to their definitions.

Then listen and repeat. 027 028

| enjoy | famous | good at | interested in |
|---|---|---|---|

______________ 1. able to do something well

______________ 2. known by many people

______________ 3. wanting to know more about something

______________ 4. like doing something

## 6 YOU DECIDE Choose an activity.

1. **Work independently.** Interview one of your classmates. Find out about the different people in your classmate's family. Make a list of what your classmate is good at, and what he or she is interested in.
2. **Work in pairs.** Imagine your family is famous. Tell your partner about the different people in your family. What are they famous for?
3. **Work in groups.** Choose one of the families from this section. Draw and illustrate their family tree.

Max Lowe

## SPEAKING STRATEGY 029

**Asking and answering personal questions**

| | |
|---|---|
| **What's** your brother's **name**? | **His name's** Lucas. |
| **What's your favourite** sport? | **My favourite** sport **is** football. |
| **Where do you live**? | **I live in** Recife. |
| **Where are** your grandparents **from**? | **They're from** Kyoto. |

1 **Listen.** How do these speakers ask and answer questions? Write the phrases you hear. 030

2 **Read and complete the dialogue.**

Gina: Is this a photo of your family?

Marco: Yes, it is.

Gina: It's a great photo.

________________ baby sister's name?

Marco: ________________ Gabriela.

Gina: And ________________ your mum from?

Marco: ________________ Rosario.

Gina: ________________?

Marco: We live in Buenos Aires.

Gina: ________________ place in Argentina?

Marco: My favourite place is Mendoza. My grandparents live there. It's really beautiful.

3 **Work in pairs.** Take turns throwing the cube. Ask and answer questions.

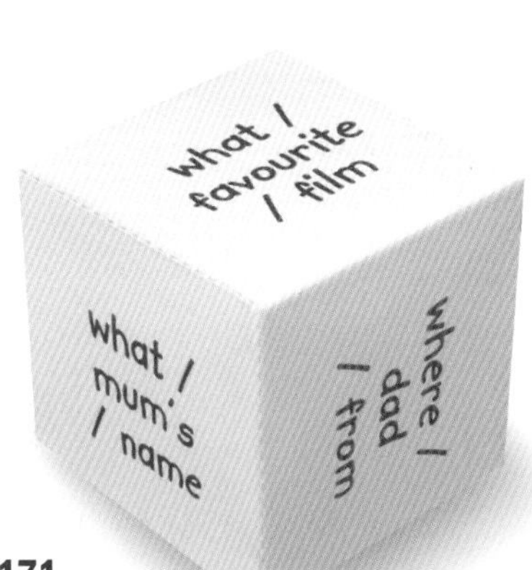


**Go to page 171.**

## GRAMMAR 031

| ***Be*** | ***Have got*** |
|---|---|
| I'**m** friendly, but my sister **isn't**. | I'**ve got** two brothers. |
| My grandparents **are** interested in photography. | My aunt **hasn't got** any children. |
| **Is** your mum good at sport? | **Have you got** any brothers or sisters? |

**1** **Listen.** You will hear six sentences about Joel's family. Circle the correct form of the verbs you hear. 032

| | | | | | |
|---|---|---|---|---|---|
| 1. | hasn't got | haven't got | 4. | 's | are |
| 2. | 'm | 's | 5. | 's got | 've got |
| 3. | is | are | 6. | isn't | aren't |

**2** **Read.** Complete the sentences with the correct form of the verbs in brackets.

Hi Petra,

This ______________ (be) a photo of my family. I ______________ (have got) one sister and one brother. We ______________ (have not got) any pets, but we ______________ (be) all interested in animals. My brother ______________ (be) really crazy about crocodiles. He ______________ (have got) crocodile posters, books and DVDs about crocodiles. His hero ______________ (be) Steve Irwin.

My sister and I ______________ (not be) crazy about crocodiles, but we love big cats. My sister ______________ (be) only four years old and she ______________ (have got) a lot of toy lions and tigers. Our house ______________ (be) next to the zoo!

How about you? ______________ (you / be) interested in animals? ______________ (you / have got) any pets?

Rita xx

**3** **LEARN NEW WORDS Listen to learn about Clare's brothers.** Then listen and repeat. 033 034

My brothers, Charlie and Peter, are very **friendly**.

Charlie is **messy** and **noisy**.

Sometimes Peter is a bit **mean** to Charlie. He thinks Charlie is **annoying**. But Charlie is really **funny**.

**4** **Work in pairs.** Describe your family. Who is messy? Who is friendly? Is anyone a bit mean sometimes?

**5** **Play a game in groups.**

1. Work together to make a list of families from your favourite books, films and TV programmes.
2. Work independently. Write a sentence about each character. Begin 'This person is ...' and use at least one word from the box below.

| | | | |
|---|---|---|---|
| **annoying** | **friendly** | **funny** | **good (at)** |
| **interested (in)** | **mean** | **messy** | **noisy** |

*This person is very good at singing.*
*This person is really funny.*

3. Read each other's sentences and try to guess the characters.

1 BEFORE YOU READ **Discuss in pairs.** Look at the title and the photo. What do you think the reading is about?

2 **LEARN NEW WORDS Find these words in the reading.** Which word is a more general word? Then listen and repeat. 035

| breakfast | dinner | lunch | meal |
|---|---|---|---|

3 WHILE YOU READ **Underline the numbers in the text.** 036

A special Saturday morning breakfast in Turkey

# BREAKFAST

## DIFFERENT WAYS TO START THE DAY AROUND THE WORLD

# IN FOUR COUNTRIES

What food does your family eat in the morning? What is your favourite breakfast food? Is your meal at breakfast very different from your meal at lunch or dinner? Do you eat the same things as your friends?

Different families around the world have got very different diets. Do you know what people have for breakfast in other parts of the world?

In Malawi, Emily, aged seven, starts the day at six in the morning. She lives with her grandmother and seven other family members. Her breakfast is porridge made from flour. She also has vegetables and drinks tea.

Oyku is nine years old. She's from Turkey. She has brown bread with olives, jam, tomatoes, eggs and a lot of different types of cheese.

Nathanaël is six and he lives in France. From Monday to Friday, Nathanaël has fruit, cereal and bread with his grandmother's homemade jam for breakfast. At the weekends he eats croissants. His favourite food, though, is pancakes (or 'crêpes' in French) with hot chocolate. In France, children drink hot chocolate from a bowl.

Viv, from the Netherlands, is five years old. She has bread with sweet sprinkles on top. This is a very popular breakfast in the Netherlands. The Dutch eat 750,000 slices of bread with chocolate sprinkles every day!

**4** AFTER YOU READ **Answer the questions.**

1. Who eats a special food at the weekend?
2. Who lives with her grandmother?
3. Who is from the Netherlands?
4. In which country do children drink from a bowl?
5. Where is Oyku from?

**5** **Work in pairs.** Find numbers in the text to complete these sentences.

1. There are ______ people in Emily's family.
2. Every day, people in the Netherlands eat __________ slices of bread with chocolate sprinkles.
3. Nathanaël is ______ years old.
4. Emily gets up at ______ in the morning.

**6** **Discuss in groups.**

1. Look at the food in the photo. Do you eat similar food? Do you want to try some of the food in the photo? Which food?
2. What do you think we can learn from the text?
3. What differences do you notice between the people in the text?

# VIDEO

1 BEFORE YOU WATCH **Discuss in pairs.** Which festivals and holidays do you celebrate together with your family? How do you celebrate them?

2 **Work in pairs.** You're going to watch *Celebrating the Dead*. Look at the photo. Why do you think the girls are smiling? Discuss your ideas.

3 WHILE YOU WATCH **Circle the things you see.** Watch scene 1.1.

| | |
|---|---|
| party hats | a book |
| a guitar | food |
| flowers | balloons |

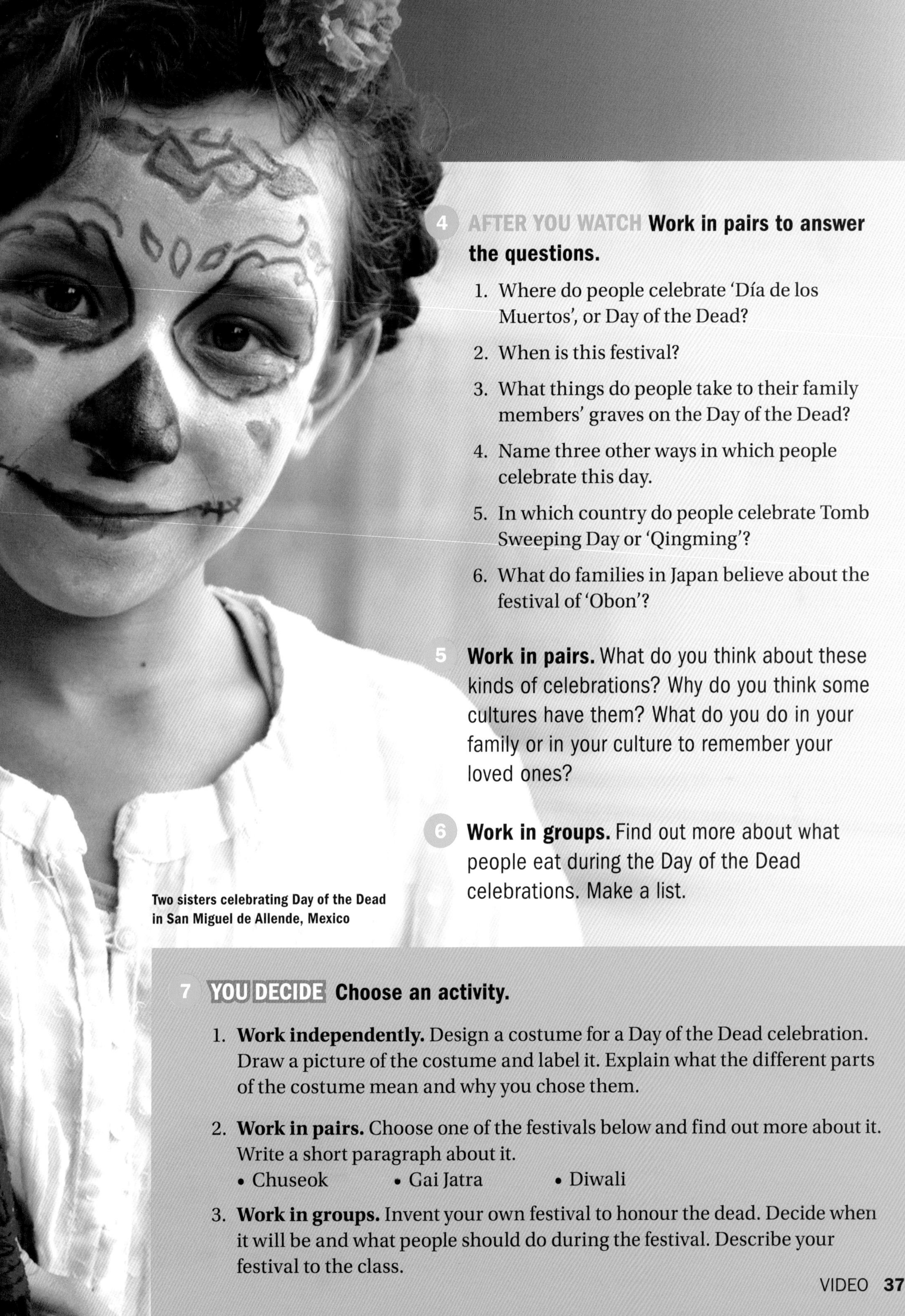

Two sisters celebrating Day of the Dead in San Miguel de Allende, Mexico

4 AFTER YOU WATCH **Work in pairs to answer the questions.**

1. Where do people celebrate 'Día de los Muertos', or Day of the Dead?
2. When is this festival?
3. What things do people take to their family members' graves on the Day of the Dead?
4. Name three other ways in which people celebrate this day.
5. In which country do people celebrate Tomb Sweeping Day or 'Qingming'?
6. What do families in Japan believe about the festival of 'Obon'?

5 **Work in pairs.** What do you think about these kinds of celebrations? Why do you think some cultures have them? What do you do in your family or in your culture to remember your loved ones?

6 **Work in groups.** Find out more about what people eat during the Day of the Dead celebrations. Make a list.

7 YOU DECIDE **Choose an activity.**

1. **Work independently.** Design a costume for a Day of the Dead celebration. Draw a picture of the costume and label it. Explain what the different parts of the costume mean and why you chose them.
2. **Work in pairs.** Choose one of the festivals below and find out more about it. Write a short paragraph about it.
   - Chuseok
   - Gai Jatra
   - Diwali
3. **Work in groups.** Invent your own festival to honour the dead. Decide when it will be and what people should do during the festival. Describe your festival to the class.

## GRAMMAR 037

**Countable and uncountable nouns**

| **Countable nouns** | **Uncountable nouns** |
| --- | --- |
| **Are there any** biscuits in the cupboard? | **Is there any** water in the bottle? |
| Yes, there are. **There are some** chocolate biscuits, but **there aren't any** ginger biscuits. | Yes, there is. And **there's some** juice in the fridge. |
| **Is there a** banana in your bag? | **Is there any** bread at the shop? |
| No, there isn't. But **there is an** apple. | No, there isn't. **There isn't any** bread, but **there's some** rice. |

1 **Listen to the conversation.** Write *C* for countable and *U* for uncountable next to each word. 038

______ kebab  ______ beefburger  ______ lettuce  ______ tomato

______ juice  ______ water  ______ banana  ______ honey

2 **Work in pairs.** Circle the correct words. Then write *some* or *any.*

Today is my sister's tenth birthday and my whole family is here for her birthday meal. There *is / are* __some__ cheese sandwiches and there *is / are* ______ crisps. There *isn't / aren't* ______ sweets because my sister doesn't like sweets, but there *is / are* ______ biscuits and there *is / are* a big chocolate cake. There *is / are* also ______ fruit – there *is / are* ______ grapes and there *is / are* ______ strawberries. There *isn't / aren't* ______ juice, but there *is / are* ______ coffee in a large pot and there *is / are* ______ water.

3 **Work in pairs.** Take turns choosing a card. Ask and answer questions using the words on the card with *Is there / Are there.*

Is there any water in the bottle?

Yes, there is.

**Go to page 173.**

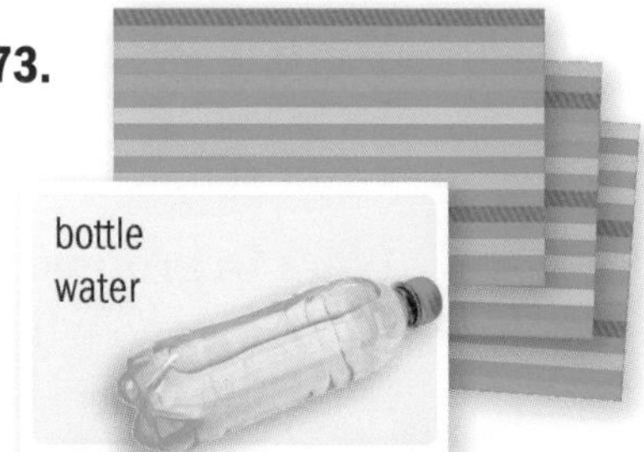

## WRITING

We use joining words, such as *and* and *but*, to connect information in a sentence. We use *and* to connect two similar pieces of information.

*She's got long hair **and** blue eyes.*

We use *but* to contrast two different pieces of information.

*My brother is very friendly, **but** my sister is quite mean.*

1 **Read the model.** How does the writer connect and contrast information? Underline the sentences with *and* and *but*.

**My Grandfather**

I've got one grandfather – my grandfather Miguel. Grandfather Miguel is from Mexico, but now he lives with us in Spain. He's 72 years old, but he's very fit and active. He's got short grey hair and brown eyes. He's quite tall and he's got a very loud voice. He's really funny and friendly. All my friends like him. His favourite meal is breakfast, and he loves the Mexican dish 'huevos rancheros' – eggs with tomatoes and chilli. He's very interested in music and he's got three guitars. He enjoys playing them, but he isn't very good at it!

2 **Work in pairs.** What information does the writer include about his grandfather? Tick the information that is in the paragraph.

______ his name ______ his personality ______ his favourite animals

______ his appearance ______ his friends ______ his interests

3 **Write.** Describe a member of your family. Remember to use *and* and *but* to connect and contrast information.

# Discover Your Values

**'The things you value in life stem from the very beginning.'**

**Max Lowe**

**National Geographic Explorer, Photographer and Writer**

1. **Watch scene 1.2.**
2. Max Lowe is from a family of climbers. He is a photographer and writer. Max travels around the world and takes photos of beautiful places. How is his career connected to his family?
3. What things are important to your family? Are they important to you? How?

# Make an Impact

**YOU DECIDE** **Choose a project.**

**1** **Draw a family tree.**

- Find out about four generations of a family.
- Draw a family tree to show how they are all in the same family.
- Write sentences about the people in the family tree. Describe the different relationships.

**2** **Make a poster about your family's breakfast.**

- Keep a record of everything your family eats for breakfast.
- Design a poster with pictures and facts about the food.
- Display your poster in the classroom. Answer your classmates' questions about the information on the poster.

**3** **Make a class family album.**

- Bring in some of your favourite family photos.
- Write a few sentences about each photo.
- Stick the photos and sentences in a book to create a class family album.

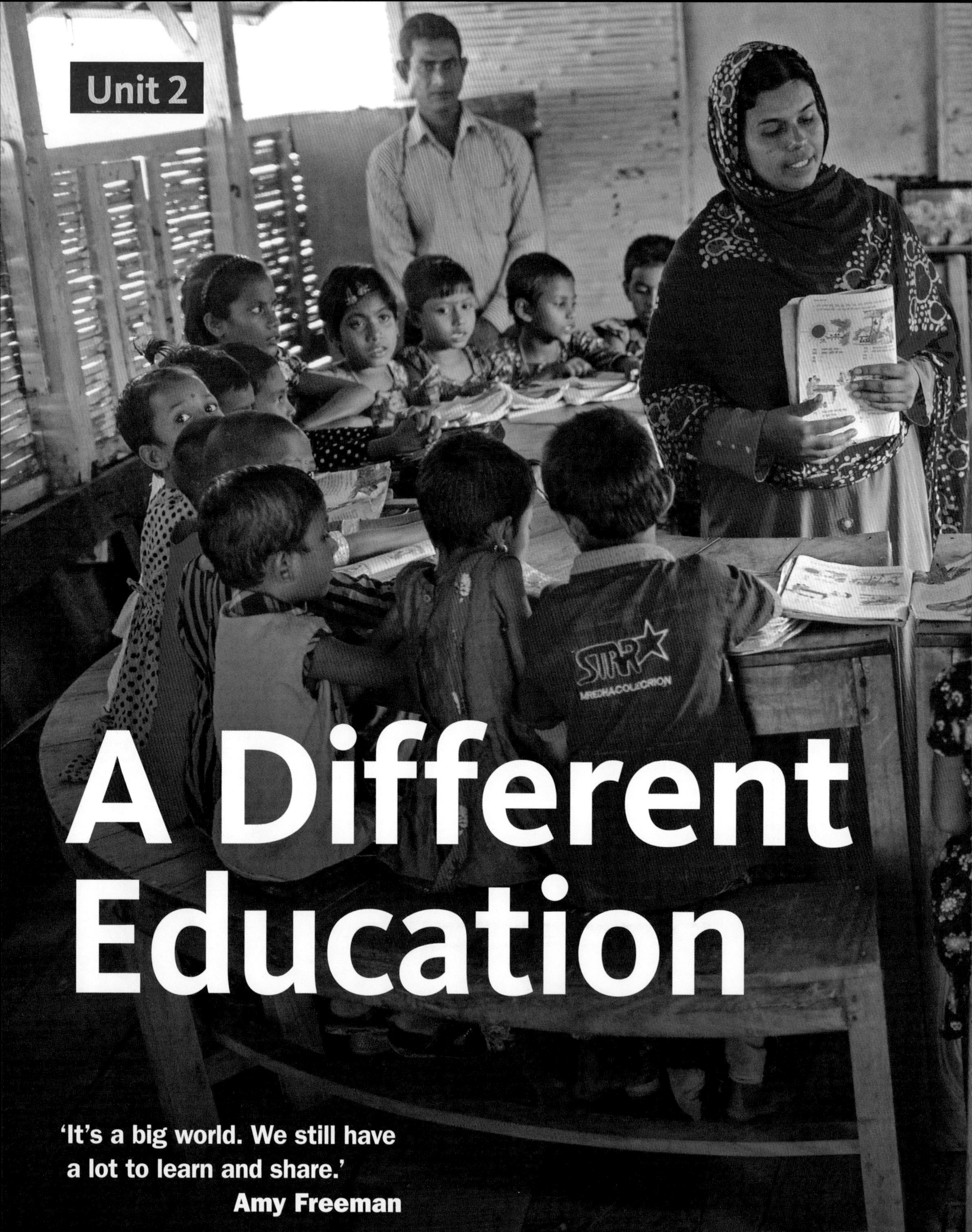

Unit 2

# A Different Education

**'It's a big world. We still have a lot to learn and share.'**
**Amy Freeman**

Children in a boat classroom, Bangladesh

## TO START

1. Look at the photo. What is unusual about this school?
2. Do you want to visit this school? Explain why or why not.
3. Imagine your perfect classroom. Where is it? Is it outside or inside? What does it look like? How many students are there?

**1** **What do you know about schools in other countries?** Discuss. Then listen and read. 039

The Nenets people are from Western Siberia. Some Nenets live in towns and villages, but many are nomadic. Nomadic people move from place to place. Nomadic Nenets follow their reindeer herds and travel around Siberia all year. They live in camps. Some Nenets children travel with their families and learn at a special nomadic school. Teachers travel with the families and the classrooms are in the camps. Some **lessons** are the same as lessons at normal schools, but in other lessons the children also learn about Nenets traditions and skills.

At an elementary school in South Korea, children have got a new English **language** teacher. It's a robot. A teacher in Australia looks into a **camera** and speaks. In their classroom in South Korea, the children hear the teacher's voice and see her face on the robot's **screen**. They follow her **instructions** and **practise** their English.

In Bangladesh, it is often difficult for children to get to school because there are problems with heavy rain. But thousands of students now have their lessons at 'floating schools'. It is easy for these students to go to school even in bad weather because 'floating schools' are on boats. There are also floating **libraries**, with a lot of books and **laptops**.

What's your classroom like? Do you get your **homework** from a robot? Do you travel with your **classmates** to a different place every week? Do you learn on the land or on the water?

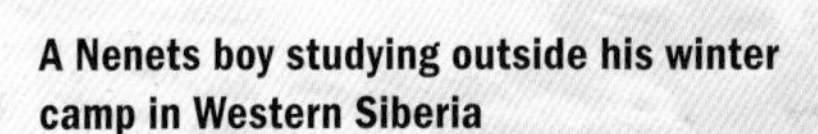

A Nenets boy studying outside his winter camp in Western Siberia

2 **LEARN NEW WORDS Listen and repeat.** 040

3 **Work in pairs.** Why do you think schools have robot teachers in South Korea? Would you like to learn from a robot teacher? Why or why not?

## 4 Read and write the words from the list.

| camera | classmate | language | laptops |
|---|---|---|---|
| lessons | library | practise | screen |

Dave and Amy Freeman are National Geographic adventurers and educators. Their Wilderness Classrooms teach children about the wild and exciting places they explore. The explorers record their adventures on a ______________________. Students then watch their videos on a ______________________ in the classroom. They can use ______________________ to send questions to the explorers. Sometimes they choose the explorers' route for the next week. The ______________________ help children to ______________________ maths, geography and science skills.

Dave and Amy Freeman dogsledding in winter

## 5 LEARN NEW WORDS Listen to these words and match them to their opposite meanings. Then listen and repeat. 041 042

| different | easy |
|---|---|
| difficult | same |

## 6 YOU DECIDE Choose an activity.

1. **Work independently.** Write three different things you want to learn at school. Explain why you want to learn about them.
2. **Work in pairs.** Design a robot teacher. Think about what it looks like and what it can do. Draw a picture of it.
3. **Work in groups.** Imagine you can choose next week's journey for Dave and Amy Freeman. What's their route?

## SPEAKING STRATEGY 043

### Talking about likes and dislikes

| | |
|---|---|
| Which subjects do you **like**? | I **like** science, but I **don't like** maths. |
| **Do you like** PE? | Yes, I do. I **love** it. |
| **Do you like** art? | No, I don't. I **hate** it. |

1 **Listen.** How do the speakers talk about their likes and dislikes? Write the phrases you hear. 044

2 **Read and complete the dialogue.**

Ahmed: What's your favourite subject at school, Haider?

Haider: ______________ geography and art. How about you? Which subjects ______________?

Ahmed: I like art, but ______________ geography. I think my favourite subject is maths.

Haider: Maths? Really? ______________ maths! I'm not very good at it.

Ahmed: ______________ science?

Haider: ______________. Science is really interesting. Do you like science?

Ahmed: ______________. It's difficult!

3 **Work in pairs.** Spin the wheel. Tell your partner about your likes and dislikes. Then ask about your partner's likes and dislikes.

I like the colours blue and black. I don't like the colour red. What colours do you like?

I like yellow and green.

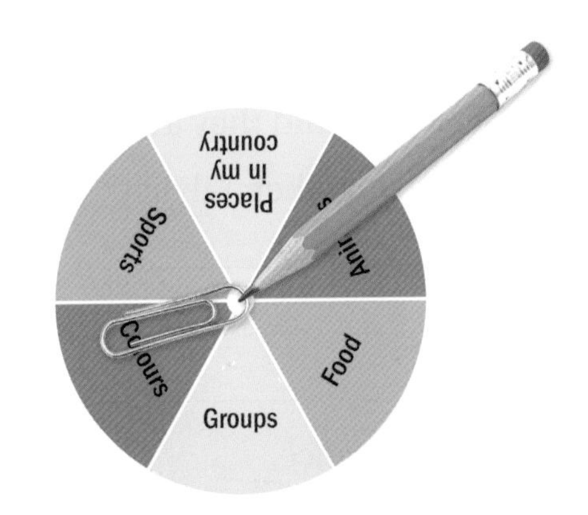


**Go to page 171.**

## GRAMMAR 045

**Present simple: Talking about routines, habits and permanent states**

Camila **lives** in Quito.

She **gets up** at six o'clock in the morning.

I **walk** to school with her.

Her brothers **don't walk** to school. They **go** by bus.

She **doesn't have** lunch at school. She **goes** home for lunch.

She **hangs out with** with her friends after lunch.

What time **does** she **go** to bed? At half past nine.

1 **Listen.** Kerem describes a typical day in his life. Circle the correct form of the verbs you hear. 046

| | | | | | |
|---|---|---|---|---|---|
| 1. | get up | gets up | 6. | doesn't have | don't have |
| 2. | eat | eats | 7. | make | makes |
| 3. | doesn't have | don't have | 8. | return | returns |
| 4. | drink | drinks | 9. | finish | finishes |
| 5. | go | goes | 10. | do | does |

2 **Read.** Complete the sentences with the correct form of the verbs in brackets.

Danilo is 12 years old and he ______________ (live) in Manila in the Philippines, with his sisters, Lilybeth and Tala, and his parents. He ______________ (get up) every morning at seven o'clock and he ______________ (prepare) breakfast for his family. After breakfast, he ______________ (start) his lessons. Danilo ______________ (not go) to school. His mother ______________ (teach) him at home in the morning. In the afternoon, he ______________ (walk) to a music lesson at his friend's house. There are five children in the music lesson and they all ______________ (practise) together. Lilybeth and Tala ______________ (not go) to the music lesson. They ______________ (stay) at home and ______________ (study) maths or science.

**3** **LEARN NEW WORDS Listen to learn about a typical school day in Japan.** Then listen and repeat. 047 048

School starts at 8.30 **on weekdays.**

The head teacher talks to the school **once a week.**

| Lesson | Time | Monday | Tuesday | Wednesday | Thursday | Friday |
|---|---|---|---|---|---|---|
| | 08.30 | Head teacher talks to the school | Class register | Class register | Class register | Class register |
| 1 | 08.45 | PE | maths | geography | maths | PE |
| 2 | 09.45 | science | geography | science | art | science |
| 3 | 10.45 | art | history | art | history | geography |
| 4 | 11.45 | history | PE | history | PE | history |
| | 12.30 | lunch | lunch | lunch | lunch | lunch |
| 5 | 1.30 | maths | science | maths | science | maths |
| | 2.30 | | After-school club | | After-school club | |

There are five lessons **every day.**

After-school clubs meet **twice a week** at the end of the school day.

There is no school **at the weekend.**

**4** **Work in pairs.** Describe your typical school week. What do you do every day? What do you do once or twice a week after school? What do you do at the weekend?

**5** **Work in groups.** Design a timetable for your ideal school. Then tell another group about your timetable.

At our school, we start lessons at half past ten every morning. We play football four times a week, and we have a maths lesson once a week.

1 **BEFORE YOU READ Discuss in pairs.** Look at the title and the photos. What do you think the reading is about?

2 **LEARN NEW WORDS Find these words in the reading.** Which words are verbs? Which word is an adjective? Then listen and repeat. 049

**fail  hard-working  improve  succeed**

3 **WHILE YOU READ Think about the main idea of the article.** 050

4 **AFTER YOU READ Answer the questions.**

1. What does Eduardo Briceño want to find out about chess champions or people who are brilliant at music or maths?
2. How does Josh Waitzkin first learn to play chess?
3. Why is his first national chess championship important for Josh?
4. What other activity is Josh also very good at?

# GROWTH MINDSET

# HOW TO BE BRILLIANT

Eduardo Briceño is an expert in education. He wants to find out why some people are chess champions or brilliant at music or maths. He believes that it is because of how they think. He calls this their 'growth mindset'. These people don't believe they are special or better than other people. They believe they can work hard and improve their skills.

One example of this is Josh Waitzkin. Let's look back at his story.

When Josh is six years old, he sees people playing chess in Washington Square Park in New York City. He learns to play chess with them. He loves the game and he plays a lot of chess! He becomes very good at it. But then, a couple of years later, he loses his first national championship.

This is an important moment for Josh. He realises that it's not about how clever you are. It's about how hard you work. He works very hard and he wins the next national championship.

Then, when he is 21 years old, Josh decides to learn something completely different. He joins a Tai Chi class. Josh works very hard again and he wins a world championship!

Josh is a great example of 'growth mindset'. He doesn't believe that he is naturally good at one special thing. He tries to learn new things. He doesn't always succeed immediately, but he is very hard-working. He thinks that it's good to fail sometimes because it makes you try harder.

We can all use 'growth mindset'. Don't think that you are good at a subject or bad at a subject. Think about how you can work hard and get better at everything you do.

**Josh Waitzkin doing Tai Chi**

**5** **Work in pairs.** What's the main idea of this reading? Underline the correct answer.

1. You can improve if you work hard.
2. Some people are very good at subjects like maths, music or chess.
3. Chess can help you to be good at other subjects.

**6** **Discuss in groups.**

1. Think of a school subject that is difficult for you. How can you improve? Share your ideas.
2. Do you think people are good at things without trying? Why or why not?
3. Eduardo Briceño says, 'Mindset affects all of us.' What do you think he means?

# VIDEO

1 BEFORE YOU WATCH **Discuss in pairs.** Look at the photo and guess. Where are the children going? How often do they make this journey?

2 **Work in pairs.** You're going to watch *Education Around the World*. From the title and the photo, predict which topics the video is about. Tick your predictions.

____ age when students start school
____ school uniform
____ journey to/from school
____ lunch breaks
____ lessons
____ school holidays
____ teachers
____ size of school

3 WHILE YOU WATCH **Check your predictions from Activity 2.** Watch scene 2.1.

4 AFTER YOU WATCH **Work in pairs.** Tick T for *True* or F for *False*.

1. Students in Finland begin school at the age of seven. T F
2. In Finland, students usually get a lot of homework. T F
3. Some students in Pennsylvania, USA, go to school by horse and cart. T F
4. Lunch breaks in French schools are usually very short. T F
5. The main summer holidays in Argentina begin in February. T F
6. Australian students have four school holidays every year. T F

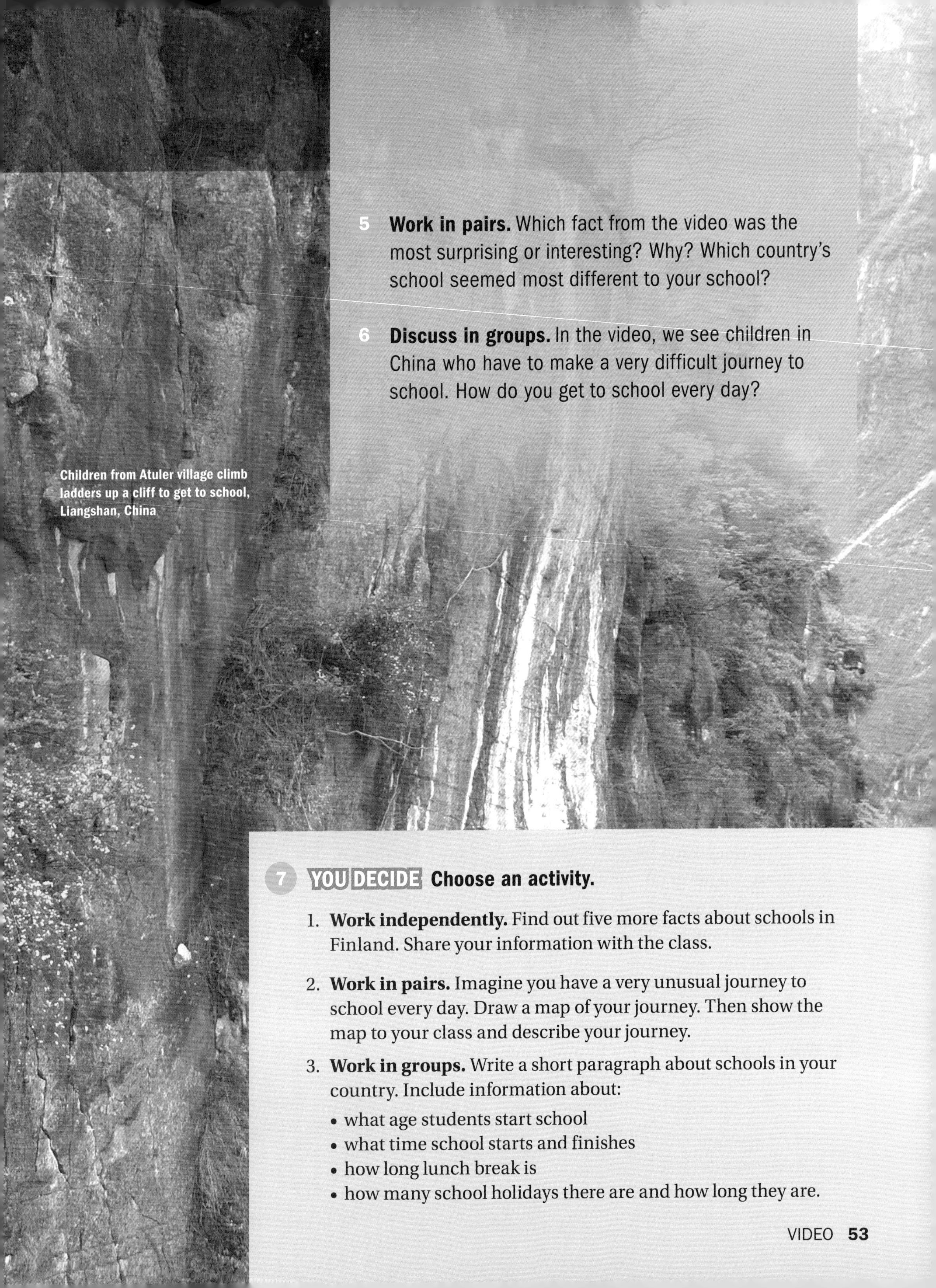

Children from Atuler village climb ladders up a cliff to get to school, Liangshan, China

5 **Work in pairs.** Which fact from the video was the most surprising or interesting? Why? Which country's school seemed most different to your school?

6 **Discuss in groups.** In the video, we see children in China who have to make a very difficult journey to school. How do you get to school every day?

7 **YOU DECIDE** **Choose an activity.**

1. **Work independently.** Find out five more facts about schools in Finland. Share your information with the class.
2. **Work in pairs.** Imagine you have a very unusual journey to school every day. Draw a map of your journey. Then show the map to your class and describe your journey.
3. **Work in groups.** Write a short paragraph about schools in your country. Include information about:
   - what age students start school
   - what time school starts and finishes
   - how long lunch break is
   - how many school holidays there are and how long they are.

## GRAMMAR 051

**Adverbs of frequency: Saying how often you do something**

0% ⟶ 100%

never | rarely | sometimes | often | always

I **never** say mean things to other people.

I **rarely** forget to do my homework.

He **sometimes** gets up at six o'clock in the morning.

She **often** has lunch at school.

We **always** report bullying to an adult.

1 **Read.** Circle the correct adverbs of frequency.

Cyberbullying – saying bad things to or about people online – is a big problem. Of course, we should *never / sometimes* post mean things online. But it is *rarely / sometimes* difficult, especially for young people. They can be very impulsive. That means they *often / never* make decisions very quickly without thinking about them carefully first. But now there is a new app called 'ReThink'. The app *always / sometimes* checks your messages before you post them. If a message is mean, the app asks, 'Do you really want to write this?' When people stop and think about a mean message, they *rarely / always* decide to post it.

**Trisha Prabhu, the inventor of the anti-cyberbullying app 'ReThink'**

2 **Work in pairs.** Discuss:

- a website you often visit
- an app you always use
- a sport you never do
- a colour you always see
- a food you sometimes eat
- a place you rarely visit
- a person you sometimes see

3 **Work in pairs.** Take turns throwing the cube. Make a sentence using the words on the cube and an adverb of frequency.

I never sing in the shower!

**Go to page 175.**

## WRITING

When we write about a person's daily routine, we use sequencing words to show the order of events:

**first** **then** **next** **before** **after**

1 **Read the model.** How does the writer show the order of events? Underline the sequencing words.

### A Day in My Life

On weekdays, I always get up at half past six in the morning. First, I have a shower, and then I have breakfast with my family. Next, I go to school. My family lives on a small island and I always go to school by boat! When the weather is very bad, I stay at home and my teacher sends me extra homework by email. School starts at 8.45 and lunch is at twelve o'clock. I often have rice with fish. After lunch, we have music or art. School finishes at three o'clock, but once a week, on Wednesday afternoon, I stay at school for football club. I really love football! I get home at four o'clock. I often go swimming in the sea before supper, and then I do my homework. I go to bed at nine o'clock. The stars are very beautiful and I can hear the sea.

2 **Work in pairs.** How similar is the writer's typical day to your day? Which things are the same? Which things are different?

3 **Write.** Describe a day in your life. Use sequencing words.

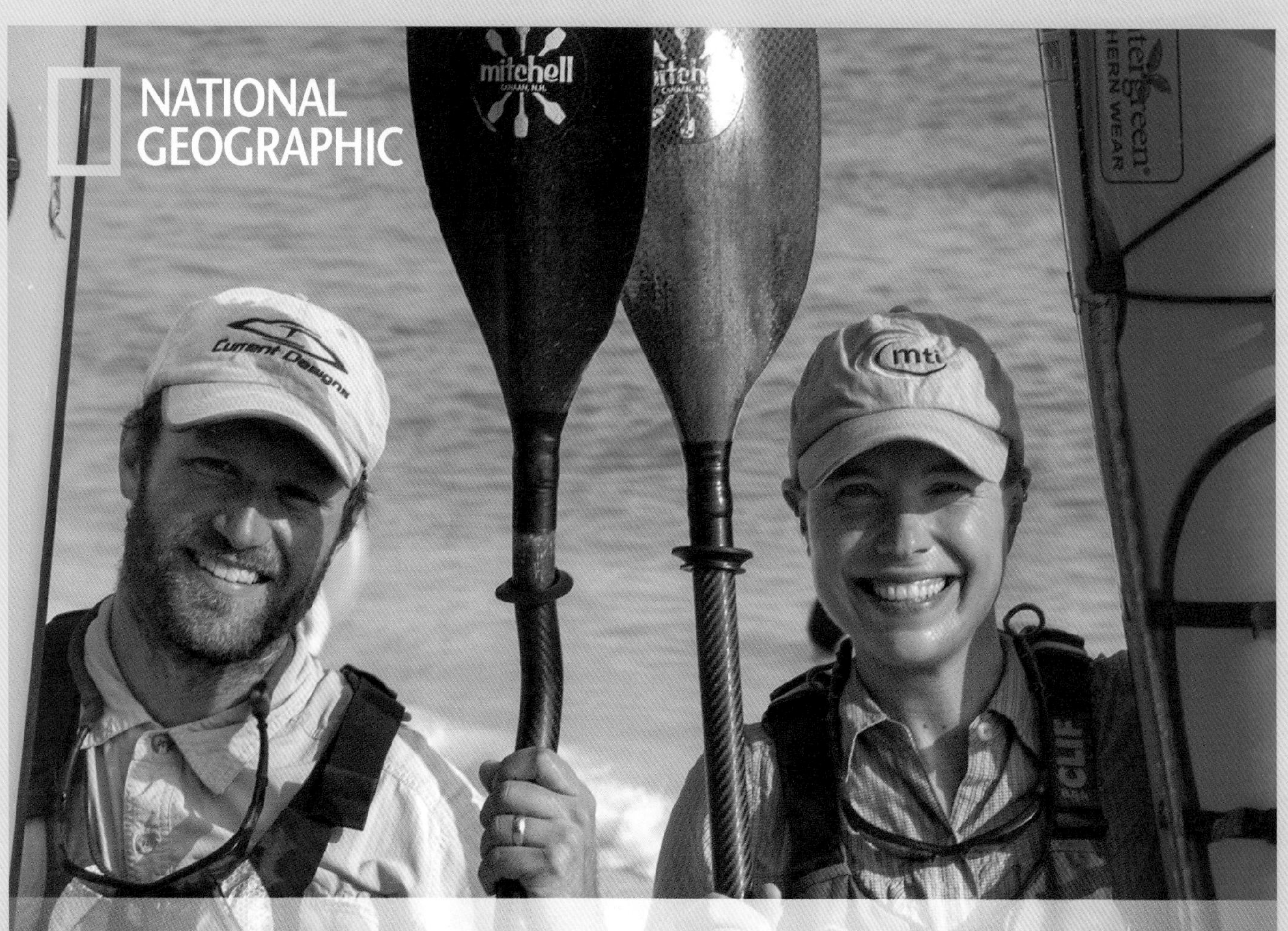


# Believe in Yourself

**'At one point I was a student sitting in a classroom just like them and I wanted to be an explorer. And now I am! And they can do it, too, if they want to.'**

**Dave Freeman**

**Dave and Amy Freeman**

**National Geographic Explorers, Adventurers and Educators**

1. **Watch scene 2.2.**
2. Dave and Amy Freeman travel around the world and tell children about their experiences. What do you think the children learn from their adventures?
3. Do you want to be an explorer? Why or why not?

# Make an Impact

**YOU DECIDE** **Choose a project.**

**1 Design your perfect school.**

- Think about the classroom, the timetable and the lessons.
- Make an advertisement for your school.
- Present your advertisement to your classmates. Do they want to join your school?

**2 Plan and do a video interview.**

- Find out about a typical school day in another country.
- Imagine you are a student in that country. Film a role-play interview about your day with a classmate.
- Show your video to your classmates and answer their questions.

**3 Make a school guide for new students.**

- Write down the most important facts about your school.
- Draw a map to show where the different classrooms are.
- Put the information together to make a leaflet about your school for new students.

# Express Yourself

**1** **Read and listen to the text messages about World Food Day.** 052

Hi, Mum. It's World Food Day at school tomorrow! Help! I have to bring some typical food from Japan. ☺

Tomorrow??

Yes, tomorrow. Sorry! The note about it is in my bag. ☹ Have you got any ideas for a typical dish from Japan?

What about some sushi? That's a typical Japanese food and it's easy to make.

That's a great idea! Can you get the ingredients for me this afternoon, please? Then we can make it when I get home from school. 😄

I'm at work this afternoon, but Grandad is always happy to help. You know he's good at cooking! You can go to the supermarket together after school.

Cool. What do we need?

You need some rice, some seaweed, a cucumber, some fish, some soy sauce and some ginger.

OK. Thanks, Mum.

Good luck making sushi!

Maki sushi

**2** **Work in groups.** Discuss the text messages.

1. What do you think students learn about at World Food Day?
2. Imagine it's World Food Day at your school. You can make a dish from any country in the world. Which country do you choose? What dish do you make?

**3** **Connect ideas.** In Unit 1, you learnt about food and families. In Unit 2, you learnt about education. What connection do you see between the two units?

**4** **YOU DECIDE** **Choose an activity.**

1. Choose a topic:
   - a family celebration
   - a school celebration
2. Choose a way to express yourself:
   - an online conversation
   - an email
   - a recipe
3. Present your work.

Unit 3

# Robots and Us

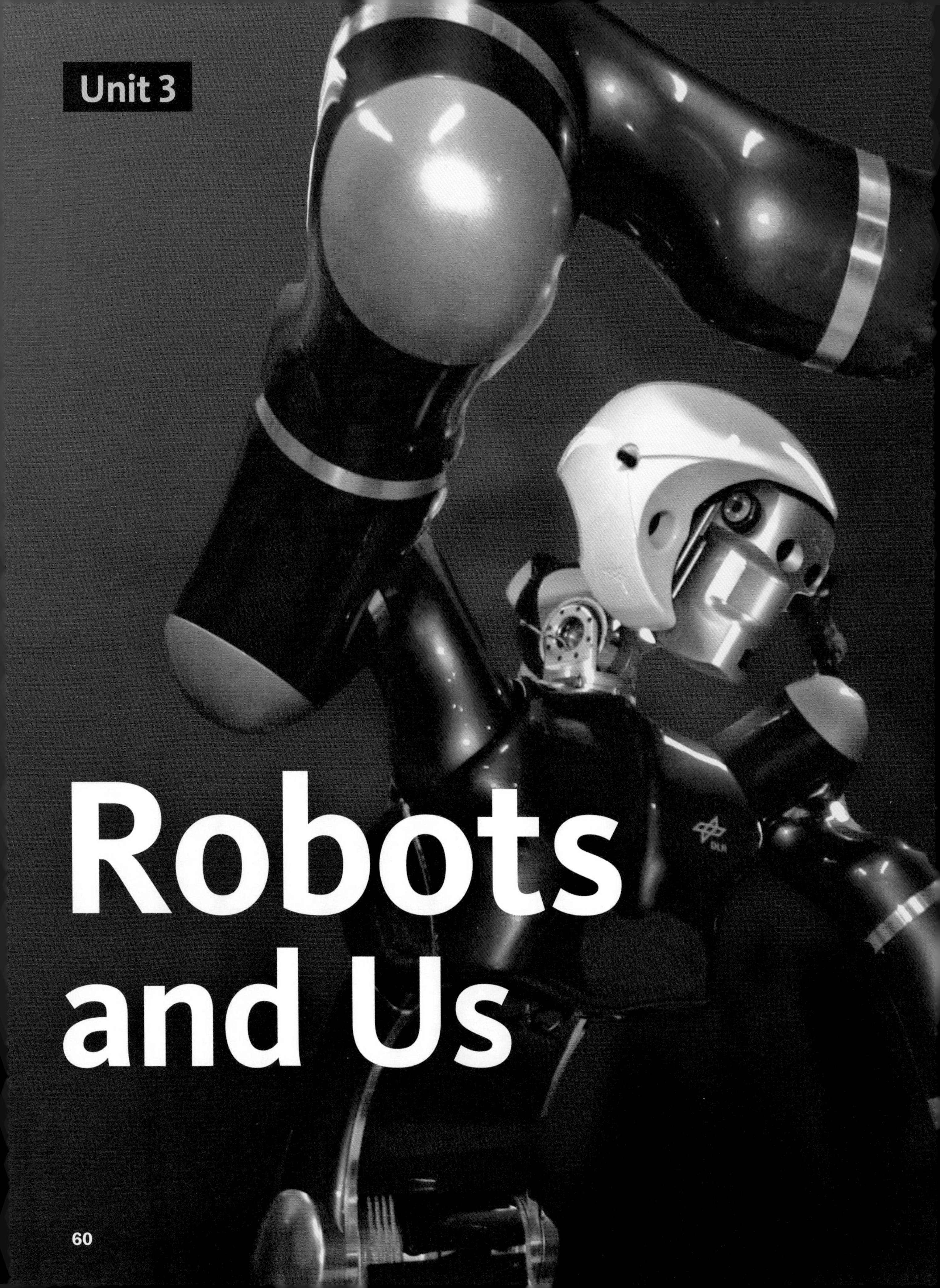

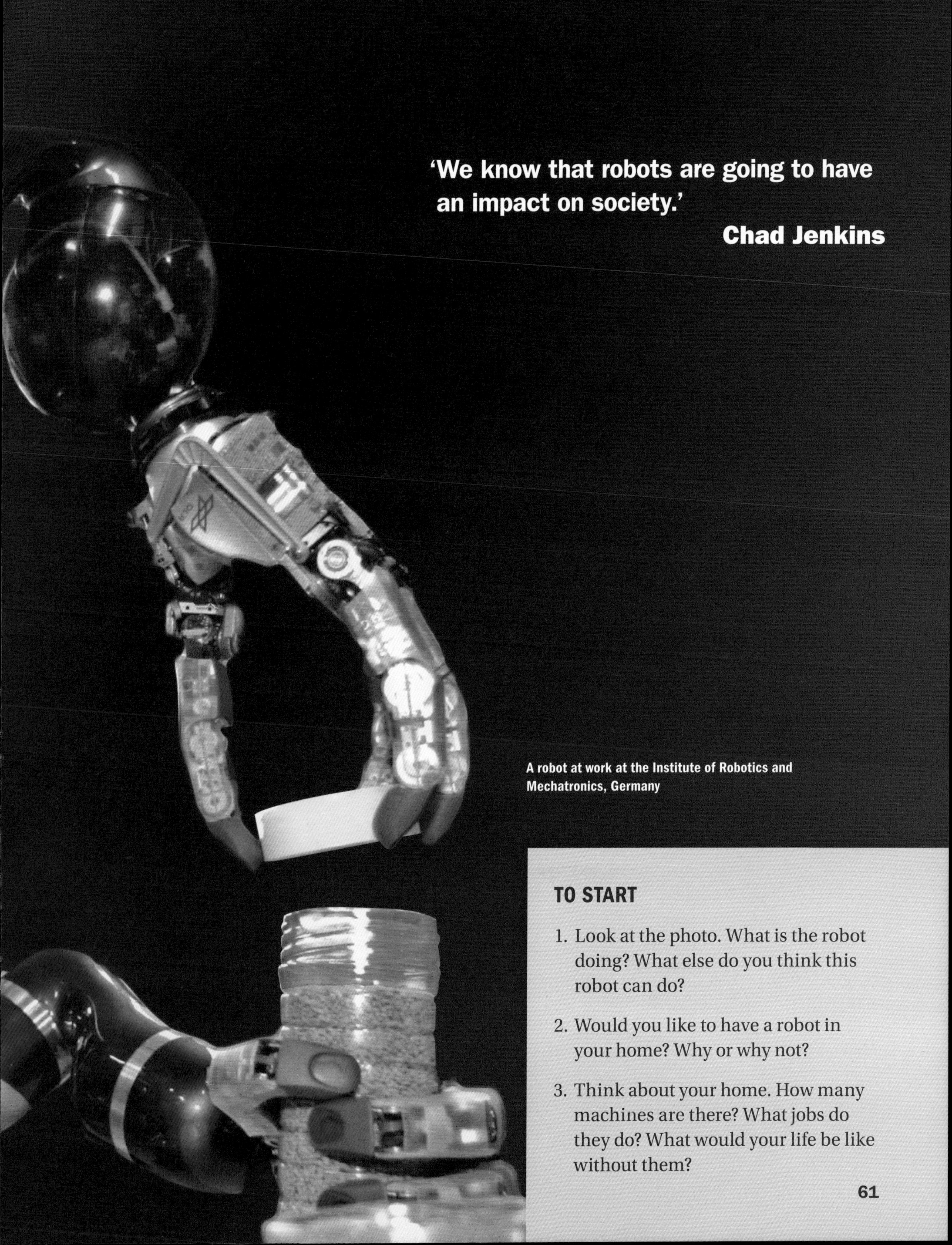

‘We know that robots are going to have an impact on society.’

**Chad Jenkins**

A robot at work at the Institute of Robotics and Mechatronics, Germany

## TO START

1. Look at the photo. What is the robot doing? What else do you think this robot can do?
2. Would you like to have a robot in your home? Why or why not?
3. Think about your home. How many machines are there? What jobs do they do? What would your life be like without them?

**1** **What do we use robots for?** Discuss. Then listen and read. 053

What do you think of when you hear the word 'robot'? Perhaps you imagine something that **follows** our instructions, brings us our clothes and **helps** us around the home. These robots do exist, but scientists also **design** many other kinds of robots for other important jobs.

**Doctors** use medical robots for surgery. They can use the robots to make very careful movements. The doctors can even **control** the robots from far away. Other doctors also use another type of robot – a therapy robot. One type of therapy robot called Paro looks and acts like a baby seal. It has got a movable head and flippers. When patients hold this robot, they feel relaxed and happy. Sometimes their **pain** levels improve.

Explorers **send** robot vehicles to places that are difficult to reach, for example, deep below the sea. They can watch the robots on a screen and control them **online** using their keyboard and **mouse**. They can decide where and when the robots move. People also use robots to do very dangerous jobs. For example, if there is a fire in a building, a robot can go into the building and look for people.

In factories, robots do a lot of very **boring** assembly line jobs. When humans do repetitive jobs – the same thing, again and again – they can make mistakes, but robots don't get bored.

A robot rescue vehicle, Russia

A child in hospital cuddling Paro, a life-like baby seal robot, Japan

**2** **LEARN NEW WORDS Listen and repeat.** 054

**3** **Work in pairs.** Design a therapy robot. What does it look like? What does it do? How does it make people feel happy? Share your ideas with the class.

## 4 Read and write the words from the list. Make any necessary changes.

| control | design | doctor | follow | help | online | send |
|---|---|---|---|---|---|---|

Chad Jenkins is a computer scientist and roboticist. He ______________ robots. He wants to teach his robots how to learn new things. A lot of people ______________ Chad to teach his robots. They visit Chad's robot lab ______________. Then they ______________ instructions to the robots. The robots ______________ the instructions. People who visit Chad's lab ______________ the robots online. They can tell the robots to play football or to do some household chores. The robots learn new things and improve because they get a lot of practice.

## 5 LEARN NEW WORDS Listen to these words and match them to their definitions. Then listen and repeat. 055 056

| bring | hold | movable | move |
|---|---|---|---|

______________ 1. change from one position to another

______________ 2. have something in your hands or arms

______________ 3. take something or someone with you to a place

______________ 4. able to change position

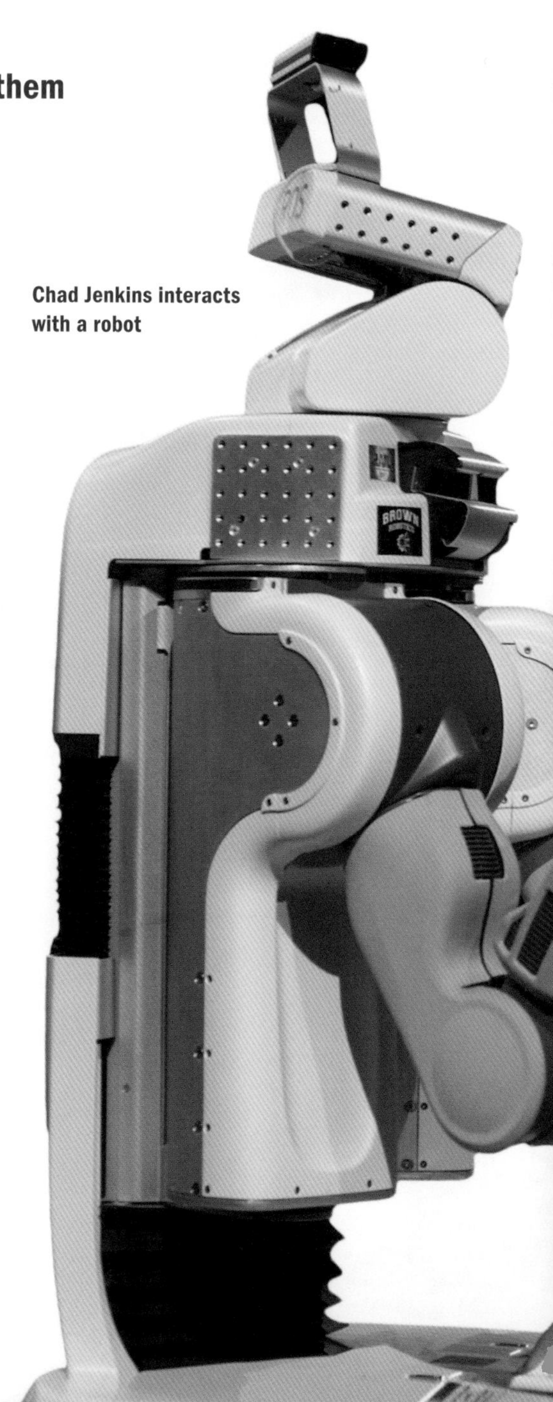

Chad Jenkins interacts with a robot

## 6 YOU DECIDE Choose an activity.

1. **Work independently.** Write a list of five instructions for the robots in Chad Jenkins' lab.
2. **Work in pairs.** Henry Evans works with Chad. He can't speak or move his arms or legs. Think of different ways a robot might help Henry.
3. **Work in groups**. Think of a very simple task for a robot, for example, 'Bring me my book.' or 'Check my email.' Then write instructions for every step of the task.

## SPEAKING STRATEGY 057

**Reacting**

| | |
|---|---|
| That's amazing! | That's boring! |
| That's fantastic! | That's a bit weird! |
| That's so cool! | That's scary! |

1 **Listen.** How do the speakers react? Write the phrases you hear. 058

2 **Read and complete the dialogue.**

Krish: There's an article in this magazine about robots.

Mariana: Robots! ______________________

Krish: No, it isn't! It's really interesting. This robot looks like a baby seal.

Mariana: Wow! ______________________

Krish: They even use them in hospitals.

Mariana: In hospitals? ______________________

Krish: Not really. The robots help patients to feel happy and relaxed.

Mariana: Really? ______________________

3 **Work in pairs.** Pick a card and react to the information on it.

**Go to page 177.**

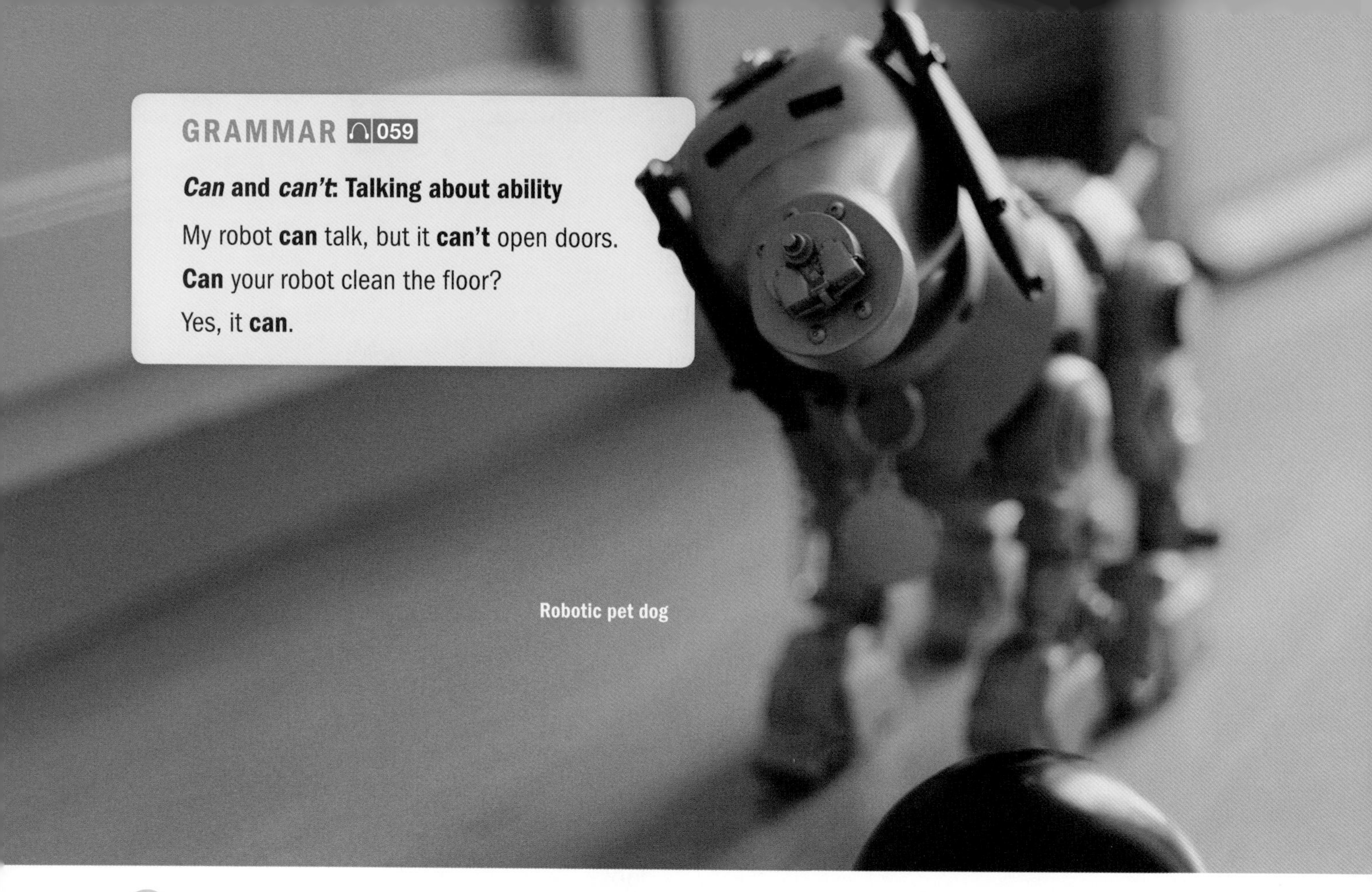


Robotic pet dog

**1** **Listen.** Tick the correct answers. 060

| | can | can't |
|---|---|---|
| jump | | ✓ |
| walk | | |
| run | | |
| load the dishwasher | | |

| | can | can't |
|---|---|---|
| go upstairs | | |
| dance | | |
| talk | | |
| understand voice instructions | | |

**2** **Work in pairs.** Imagine you have got a robot. Think of five things it can do and five things it can't do. You can use the ideas in the box below or your own ideas. Then compare your robot with another pair's robot.

| | | | | |
|---|---|---|---|---|
| **hold things** | **run** | **jump** | **swim** | **talk** |
| **laugh** | **sing** | **load the dishwasher** | **clean the house** | **play football** |
| **dance** | **drive a car** | **read a book** | **understand voice instructions** | |

Our robot can hold things and it can dance, but it can't sing. Can your robot sing?

Yes, it can. Our robot can sing and it can run, but it can't understand voice instructions.

**3** **LEARN NEW WORDS Listen to learn about what robots can and can't do.** Then listen and repeat. 061 062

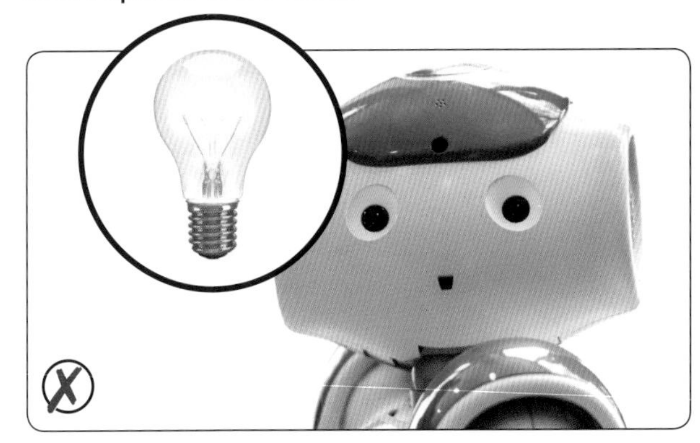

Robots can't **imagine** things.

Humans can feel sad and **cry**.

Humans can feel happy and **laugh**.

Robots can't **dream**.

**4** **Work in pairs.** Complete these sentences about yourself. Then compare your answers with your partner.

I sometimes dream about ...

I like to imagine I'm ...

I laugh when ...

I cry when ...

**5** **Work in groups.** What do you think these robots can do? What can't they do? Complete the sentences below with your own ideas.

A fast-food restaurant robot *can prepare food and it can do the washing up. It can talk to people. It can't laugh and it can't use a computer.*

A hospital robot ______________________________

______________________________

A school robot ______________________________

______________________________

A police robot ______________________________

______________________________

1 BEFORE YOU READ **Discuss in pairs.** Look at the title and the photo. What do you think the reading is about?

2 **LEARN NEW WORDS Find these words in the reading.** Use the other words around them to guess their meaning. Then listen and repeat. 063

| | |
|---|---|
| **code** | **program** |
| **engineering** | **project** |

3 WHILE YOU READ **Think about the main point of each paragraph.** 064

4 AFTER YOU READ **Look at the sentences.** Tick T for *True* or F for *False*.

1. Boys aren't better than girls at maths and science at school. T F
2. Many girls study computer science at university. T F
3. Reshma Saujani works as an engineer. T F
4. 'Girls Who Code' is an after-school club organisation. T F
5. Girls can make computers at 'Girls Who Code' clubs. T F
6. A lot of girls want to study computer science or engineering at university because of 'Girls Who Code' clubs. T F

# How to Change the Future

Boys and girls are both good at science and maths at school. But there is a big 'gender divide' in subjects like computer science and engineering at university. A 'gender divide' means there is a difference between what girls do and what boys do. Very few girls study computer science or engineering at university and very few girls get jobs in these subject areas. In fact, only 20% of engineering graduates and only 18% of computer science graduates in the USA are girls.

Computer science and engineering are useful and interesting subjects. Engineers use science and maths to create and design things. Computer scientists work on new computer programs. So how can we get more girls to study these subjects?

Reshma Saujani is an American lawyer. She wants to change things. Her organisation, 'Girls Who Code', runs after-school clubs and summer schools all around the USA. The clubs are free, and they teach girls how to write code, or special instructions, for computers. The girls use these instructions to make basic computer programs. They work on projects together to help their community.

The clubs are a big success. There are now 10,000 girls in 'Girls Who Code' after-school clubs around the USA. Many of these girls want to study computer science or engineering when they leave school.

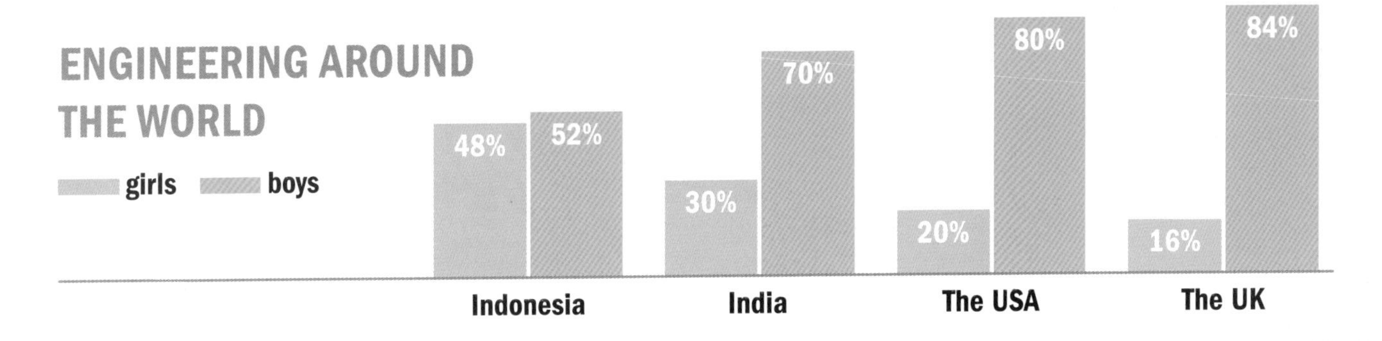


**5** **Work in pairs.** Write the correct paragraph number for the descriptions below.

_____ An explanation of computer science and engineering.

_____ The effect of the 'Girls Who Code' clubs.

_____ An introduction to the topic.

_____ A description of the 'Girls Who Code' clubs.

**6** **Discuss in groups.**

1. Do you think there are any subjects that girls are better at or that boys are better at? Why or why not?
2. Why do you think STEM subjects (science, technology, engineering and maths) are less popular with girls? How can we change that?
3. Imagine you can organise some after-school clubs around your area. What clubs do you want to organise? Why do you want to organise these clubs? Who will join them?

# VIDEO

1 **BEFORE YOU WATCH Discuss in pairs.** How can robots help explorers in places that are very dangerous or difficult to reach?

2 **Work in pairs.** You are going to watch *Squishy Robot Fingers*. Before you watch, look at the photo. What do you think it shows? What is it doing?

3 **WHILE YOU WATCH Check your answers from Activity 2.** Were they correct? What else did you learn about Squishy Fingers? **Watch scene 3.1.**

4 **AFTER YOU WATCH Work in pairs.** Circle the correct words.

1. David Gruber first tested Squishy Fingers in a *swimming pool / coral reef* .
2. Now he is testing it *in a boat / on a coral reef* .
3. Squishy Fingers is made from *metal / rubber* .
4. David's old robots were designed for *coral / oil exploration* .
5. Squishy Fingers grabs a *small / large* piece of coral.
6. David and the team are *happy / unhappy* with the test.

5 **Work in pairs.** Compare Squishy Fingers' hands with the older robot hands. Draw a table with three headings: *Task*, *Squishy Fingers* and *Older Robot Hands*. Tick which robot could do each task better.

Squishy Fingers in action underwater

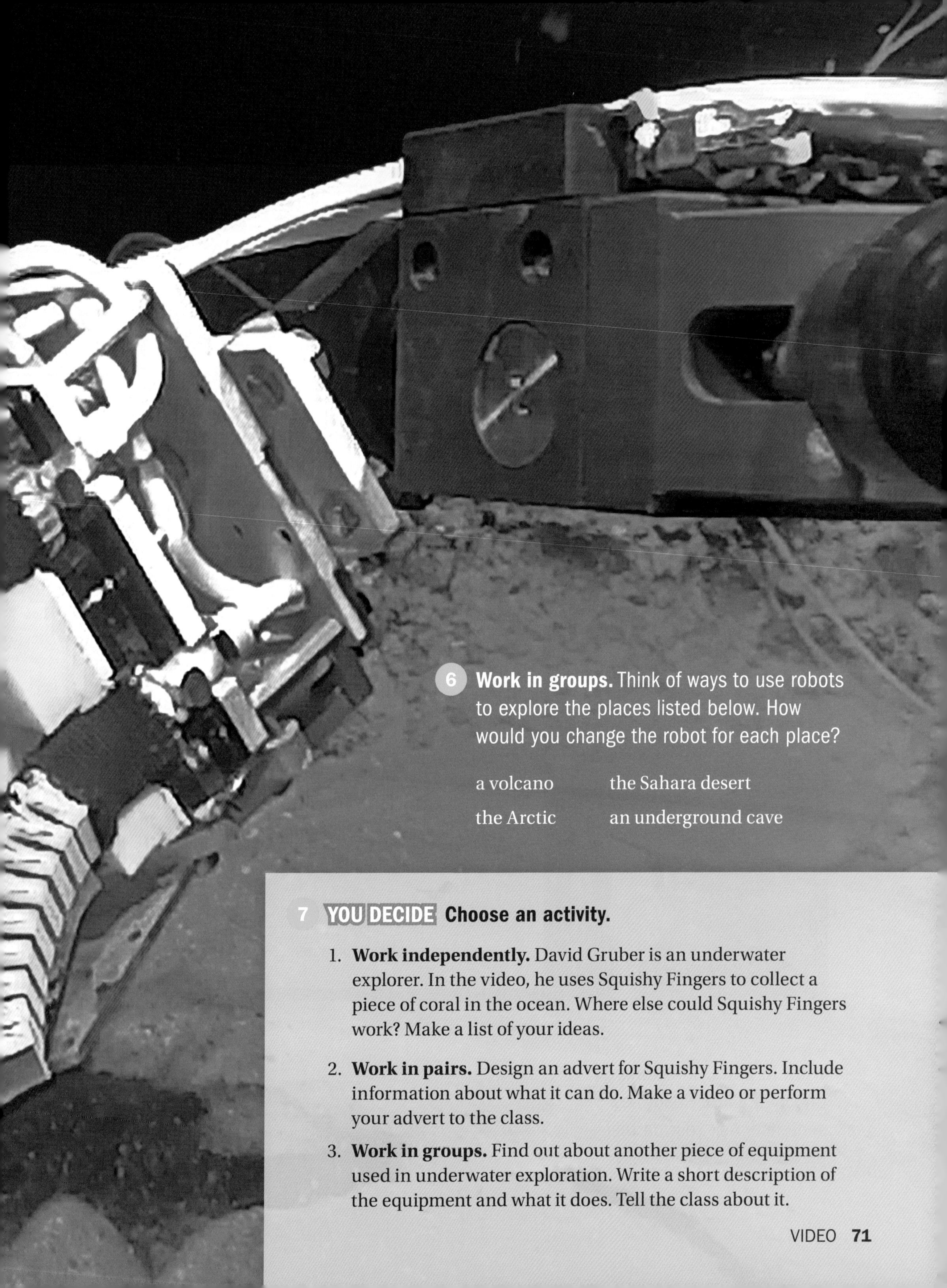

6 **Work in groups.** Think of ways to use robots to explore the places listed below. How would you change the robot for each place?

| | |
|---|---|
| a volcano | the Sahara desert |
| the Arctic | an underground cave |

7 **YOU DECIDE Choose an activity.**

1. **Work independently.** David Gruber is an underwater explorer. In the video, he uses Squishy Fingers to collect a piece of coral in the ocean. Where else could Squishy Fingers work? Make a list of your ideas.
2. **Work in pairs.** Design an advert for Squishy Fingers. Include information about what it can do. Make a video or perform your advert to the class.
3. **Work in groups.** Find out about another piece of equipment used in underwater exploration. Write a short description of the equipment and what it does. Tell the class about it.

## GRAMMAR 065

***Should* and *shouldn't*: Giving advice**

We **should** join the after-school coding club.

You **shouldn't** buy this robot. It's very expensive.

They **should** study for this maths test.

**1** **Read.** Use *should* or *shouldn't* with the correct verb from the box to complete the sentences.

| forget | join | learn | look | read | spend | start | study | watch |
|---|---|---|---|---|---|---|---|---|

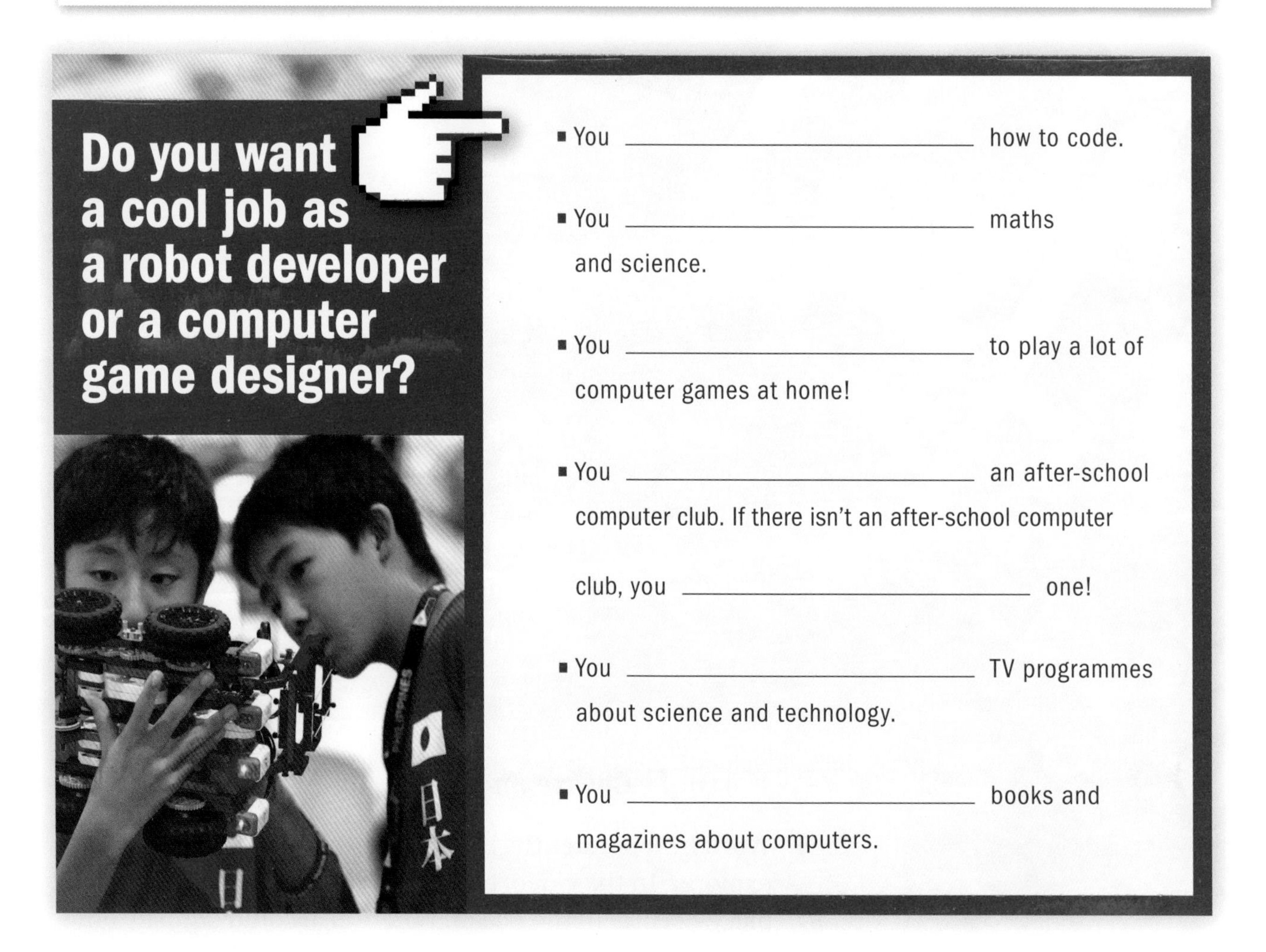


- You ______________________ how to code.
- You ______________________ maths and science.
- You ______________________ to play a lot of computer games at home!
- You ______________________ an after-school computer club. If there isn't an after-school computer club, you ______________________ one!
- You ______________________ TV programmes about science and technology.
- You ______________________ books and magazines about computers.

**2** **Work in pairs.** Take turns. Choose a card. Read the sentence. Ask your partner for advice.

You should ask your maths teacher for help.

**Go to page 179.**

## WRITING

When we contrast two different things, we use words like *but* and *however.* We can use *however* at the beginning of a sentence.

*Your robot is very strong,* ***but*** *it isn't very intelligent.*
*My robot cleans the floor.* ***However,*** *it can't open the door.*

1 **Read the model.** How does the writer contrast information? Underline the words that show contrast.

Buddy and Sega™ Toys Dream Cat are both robots, but they're very different. Buddy is a companion robot. He's got three wheels and he's got a screen for a face. However, he hasn't got moveable arms, so he can't bring things to you and he can't wash your dishes! He can check your emails and he can wake you up in the morning, but he's very expensive. Sega™ Toys Dream Cat is a robot pet. She can't check your emails or wake you up in the morning, but she is very cute! She can purr and she can move her tail. However, she can't walk or run. Which robot do you prefer?

Buddy the robot

Sega™ Toys Dream Cat

2 **Work in pairs.** Find two things Buddy can do and two things he can't do. Find two things Sega™ Toys Dream Cat can do and two things she can't do.

3 **Write.** Compare two different gadgets in your house, for example, a smartphone and a computer. Think about what they're like, what they can do and what they can't do. Use *but* and *however* to show contrast.

# Change the World

**'We provide the technology so that you can help us to reach out and change the world.'**

**Chad Jenkins**
**National Geographic Explorer, Computer Scientist and Roboticist**

1. **Watch scene 3.2.**
2. Chad Jenkins develops new types of robots. How do you think they can help change the world?
3. Imagine you can use technology to change your town or country. What technology do you use? How does it change your town or country?

# Make an Impact

**YOU DECIDE** **Choose a project.**

**1** **Prepare a presentation about a famous robot.**

- Find out facts about a famous robot – fictional or real.
- Find photos and illustrations of the robot.
- Give a presentation about the robot to the class.

**2** **Design your own robot.**

- Think about what your robot can and can't do.
- Draw a picture of your robot and label it.
- Display your picture in the class. Answer your classmates' questions about it.

**3** **Write a Coding Club Invitation.**

- Decide when the club will be and what students will learn.
- Include information about why learning to code is important.
- Send your Coding Club Invitation to your classmates.

**C-3PO and R2D2 from *Star Wars: Episode III Revenge of the Sith***

Unit 4

# Part of Nature

Butterflies on the shoreline of the Juruena River, Brazil

'We are part of nature and the ecosystem, not something separate.'
**Juliana Machado Ferreira**

## TO START

1. Look at the photo and read the caption. What kinds of animals live in this place? Would you visit here? Why or why not?
2. How are you 'part of nature'? What do you think nature and wild animals can teach us?
3. Do you sometimes visit zoos or wildlife parks? Which animals do you see there?

**1 What do you know about giant pandas?**
Discuss. Then listen and read. 066

Did you know that almost 7,000 different types of animals are **endangered**? Fortunately, there are some amazing wildlife **conservation** projects around the world.

Thanks to conservation projects, giant **pandas** are not endangered anymore, but they still need our help. There are now 1,800 pandas in the **wild**, and the panda population is growing slowly. Thirty per cent of the world's population of giant pandas lives in the Sichuan Giant Panda Sanctuaries in China. These sanctuaries are famous for their work with giant pandas and with other endangered animals, including snow leopards and red pandas.

There are seven nature reserves in a very big **area** of land in the sanctuaries. Here, giant pandas can live safely in the wild. Their favourite food, bamboo, **grows** in the **forests** around the mountains.

Increasing the giant panda population is a very important part of the sanctuaries' conservation work. At a special research centre, **workers** keep some pandas in **captivity** for breeding. When the baby pandas are born, the workers help the mothers to look after them. They try to teach them how to live in the wild. They don't want the pandas to be too friendly with people, so the workers wear panda **costumes**!

With a combination of conservation, research, science and some very cute costumes, the Sichuan Giant Panda Sanctuaries are continuing to help to bring giant pandas back into the wild.

A worker wearing a panda costume, Wolong, Sichuan Province, China

**2** LEARN NEW WORDS **Listen and repeat.** 067

**3** **Work in pairs.** Why do you think the workers don't want the baby pandas to be too friendly with people?

## 4 Read and write the words from the list.

| area | captivity | conservation | endangered | forest | wild | worker |
|---|---|---|---|---|---|---|

National Geographic Explorer Juliana Machado Ferreira is a conservation biologist. She works on ______________ projects in Brazil. There is a big problem in Brazil because people take ______________ birds from their homes in the ______________ and then sell them as pets. Because of this, some of these birds are now ______________. Juliana wants to teach people that when you keep these birds in ______________, it's very bad for nature. She uses her knowledge of biology to find out which ______________ the birds originally come from, and then she returns the birds to their homes.

Juliana Machado Ferreira

## 5 LEARN NEW WORDS Listen to these words and match them to their definitions. Then listen and repeat. 068 069

| leopard | mountain | reserve | wildlife |
|---|---|---|---|

______________ 1. a place where the animals and plants are protected

______________ 2. animals and plants that live in a natural environment

______________ 3. a large wild animal of the cat family

______________ 4. a very high hill

## 6 YOU DECIDE Choose an activity.

1. **Work independently.** Why is it a bad idea to own a wild animal as a pet? Think of three reasons. Share your ideas with the class.
2. **Work in pairs.** Imagine you work at the Sichuan Giant Panda Sanctuaries research centre. What do you like about your work? What parts of your work are difficult?
3. **Work in groups.** Design an advertisement for the Sichuan Giant Panda Sanctuaries.

## SPEAKING STRATEGY 070

### Checking facts

| | |
|---|---|
| There are seven nature reserves in the Sichuan Giant Panda Sanctuaries. | **Really**? |
| Yes. The most famous is the Wolong Nature Reserve. | **How big** is it? |
| It's 2,000 square kilometres. | **How many** pandas are there? |
| I don't know exactly. I think there are about 100. | **Are there really** 100 pandas there? |
| I think so! | |

1 **Listen.** How do the speakers check information? Write the phrases you hear. 071

2 **Read and complete the dialogue.**

Samira: Hey, look at these cute baby panda pictures! They're from the research centre in Sichuan, China. The workers wear panda costumes.

Hadil: ________________________ ?

Samira: Yes, look!

Hadil: ________________________ baby pandas are at the research centre?

Samira: There are 16 babies.

Hadil: ________________________ 16 baby pandas there?

Samira: Yes, there are. It's a very successful centre.

Hadil: ________________________ is it?

Samira: I don't know, but the Sichuan Giant Panda Sanctuaries reserve is very big. It covers 9,245 square kilometres.

3 **Work in pairs.** Take turns. Choose an information card. Give the matching picture card to your partner. Answer your partner's questions about the nature reserve on your information card.

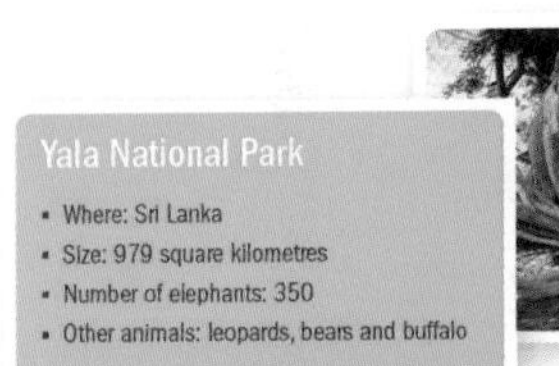

**Go to page 181.**

## GRAMMAR 072

**Quantifiers: Talking and asking about quantity**

**How many** different kinds of camels are there?

There are two kinds of camels.

**How much** food do they eat every day?

**A lot**! Camels eat **a lot** of cacti and dry plants.

There is very **little** grass and there are very **few** plants in the desert.

1 **Read.** Use *how much, how many, a lot, little* and *few* to complete the fact sheet.

### Camels: FAQs

______________ humps has a camel got?

Well, it depends. Dromedary camels have got one hump and Bactrian camels have got two humps.

______________ water can a camel drink?

______________ ! There is very ______________ water in the desert.

When a camel finds water, it can drink ______________ !

______________ wild Bactrian camels are there in the world?

There are very ______________ wild Bactrian camels. There are only about 1,000 in the wild. They are endangered.

2 **Work in pairs.** Write two more questions about camels with *how much* or *how many*. Then do some research to find out the answers. Share your answers with the class.

How ______________________________________________?

How ______________________________________________?

An Afar camel caravan crosses the salt flats of Lake Assal, Djibouti

3 **LEARN NEW WORDS Listen and read to learn about camels.** Then listen and repeat. 073 074

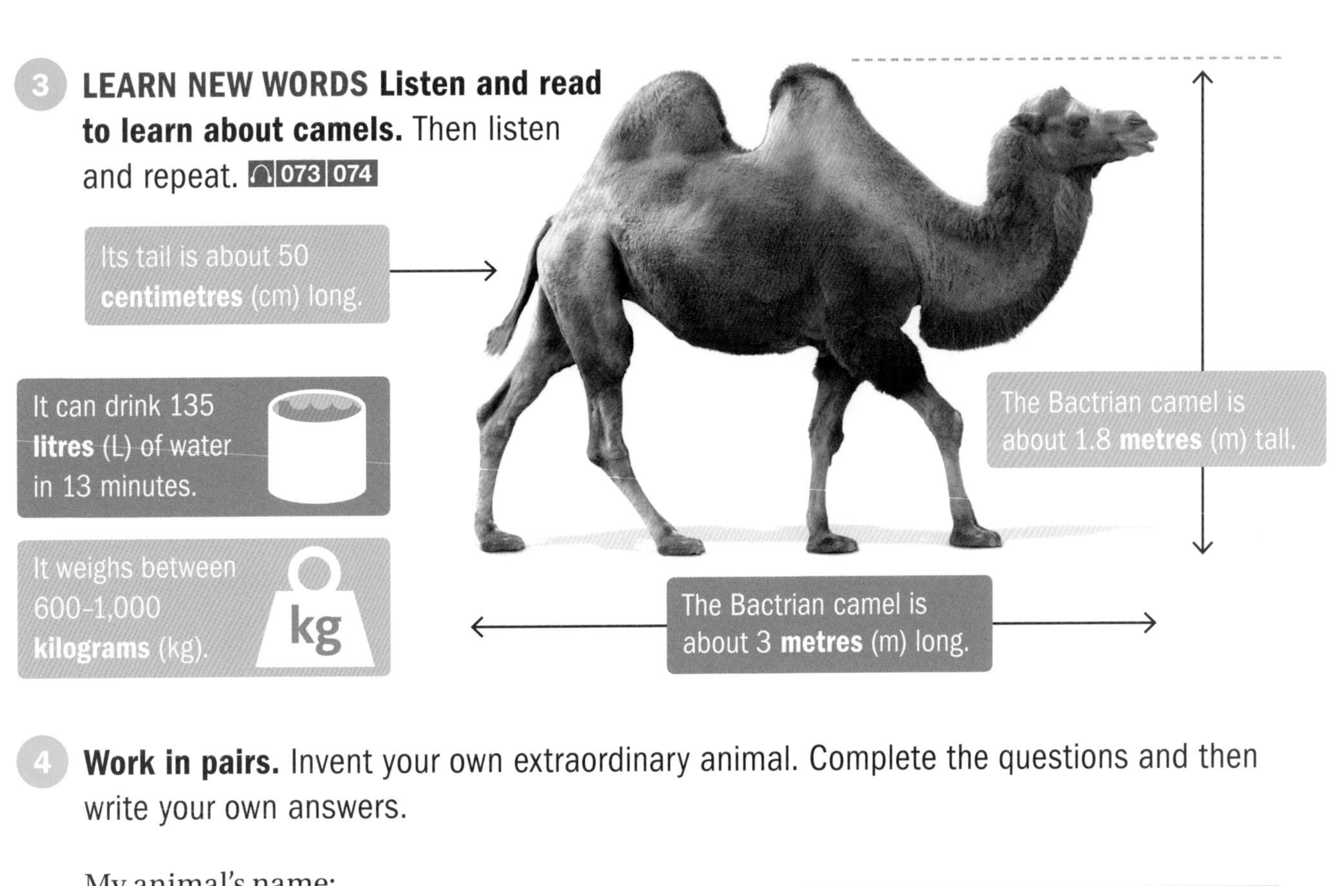


4 **Work in pairs.** Invent your own extraordinary animal. Complete the questions and then write your own answers.

My animal's name: ____________________

How tall ____________________? → It is ____________________ tall.

How much ____________________? → It weighs ____________________.

How much ____________________? → It drinks ____________________ of water in ____________________ minutes.

How far ____________________? → It can walk ____________________ in ____________________ day(s).

5 **Work in groups.** Ask other students about their amazing animal.

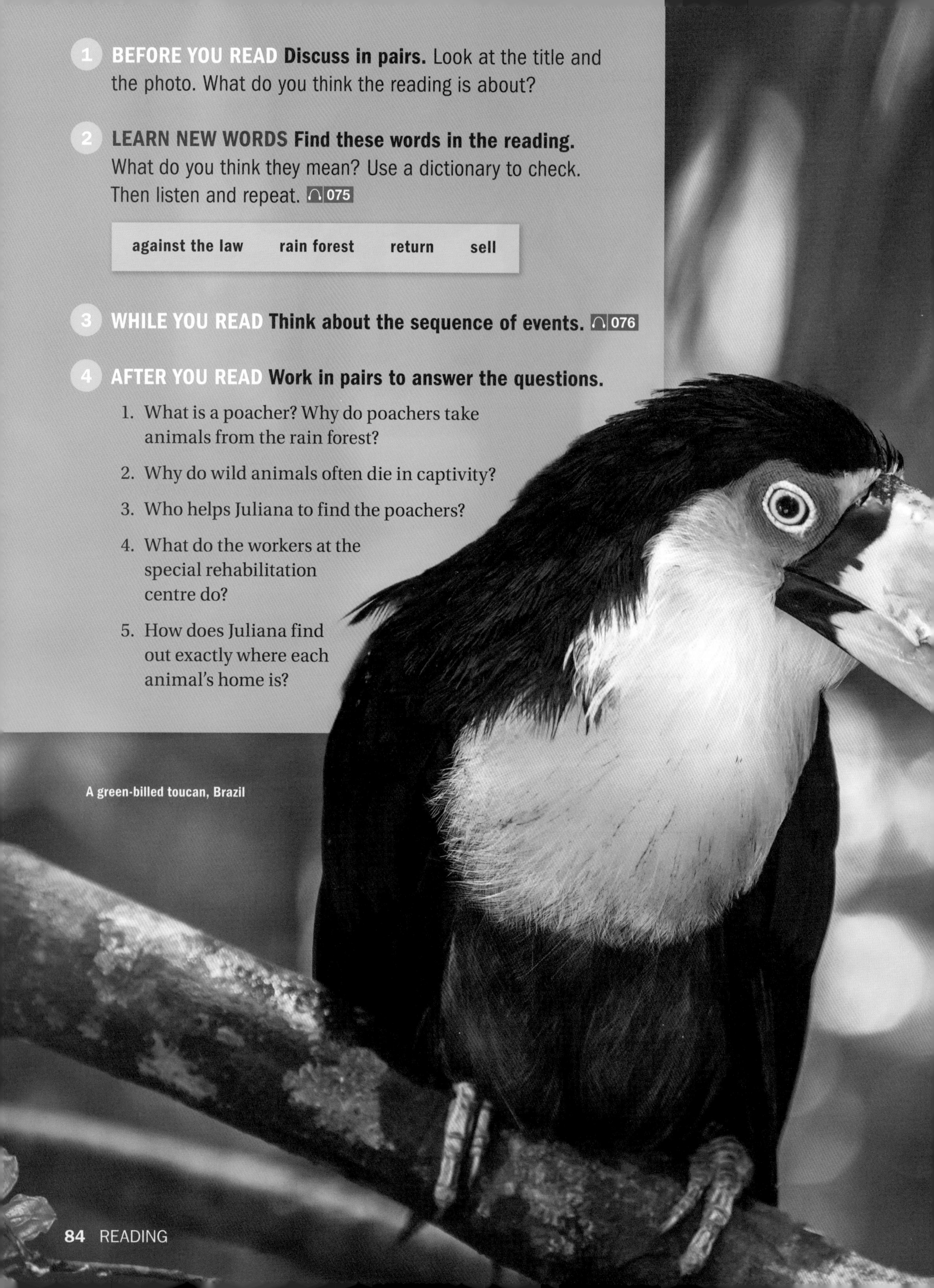

1 **BEFORE YOU READ Discuss in pairs.** Look at the title and the photo. What do you think the reading is about?

2 **LEARN NEW WORDS Find these words in the reading.** What do you think they mean? Use a dictionary to check. Then listen and repeat. 075

**against the law** **rain forest** **return** **sell**

3 **WHILE YOU READ Think about the sequence of events.** 076

4 **AFTER YOU READ Work in pairs to answer the questions.**

1. What is a poacher? Why do poachers take animals from the rain forest?
2. Why do wild animals often die in captivity?
3. Who helps Juliana to find the poachers?
4. What do the workers at the special rehabilitation centre do?
5. How does Juliana find out exactly where each animal's home is?

A green-billed toucan, Brazil

# A WILD ANIMAL ISN'T A PET

## RETURNING WILD ANIMALS TO THE RAIN FOREST

Every year in Brazil, people take millions of animals from the rain forest and sell them as pets. These people are called poachers. This is against the law, but people love to buy these beautiful animals and keep them as pets. In fact, people in Brazil spend more than £1.5 billion every year on birds, turtles, lizards and other wild pets. However, the animals are not happy in captivity. People don't know how to care for them. The animals often die because they eat the wrong food or because they are very unhappy. Wild animals have an important role in nature. If people take them from their homes in the wild, it can cause problems for other wildlife.

Juliana Machado Ferreira works together with the police to find the poachers and to save the animals. She then takes them to a special centre where workers look after the animals. They teach the animals how to find food in the wild. The birds learn how to fly again. When they are ready, the animals can return to the rain forest.

Juliana now has another important job. She wants to find out exactly where each animal's home is in the rain forest. But the rain forest in Brazil is a very big place. Juliana looks at the animals' DNA. This gives her important information about each animal and its home. Then, at last, she can take the animals back to the right places in the rain forest.

5 **Work in pairs.** Put these events into the correct order.

_____ Workers at the centre help the animals to learn important skills.

_____ The animals return to the rain forest.

_____ Juliana and the police save the wild animals from the poachers.

_____ Juliana takes the wild animals to a special centre.

_____ Poachers take wild animals from the rain forest.

_____ Juliana looks at the animals' DNA.

6 **Discuss in groups.**

1. Does the reading change your opinion about wild animals as pets? Explain why or why not.
2. Why do you think it's important for the animals to return to exactly the same place in the rain forest? Think of several different reasons.
3. Do you think it's important to learn about the wild animals from your own country? Why or why not?

# VIDEO

**1** BEFORE YOU WATCH **Discuss in pairs.** What do you already know about pandas? Remember what you read about pandas on page 78. Try to answer these questions together:

1. In which country do many giant pandas live?
2. How many giant pandas are there in the wild?
3. What food do giant pandas love to eat?

**2** **Read and circle.** You are going to watch *Into the Real Wild: Photographing Pandas with Ami Vitale*. From the title, predict what the video is about. Circle the letter.

a. Returning pandas to the wild
b. Looking for pandas in the wild

**3** WHILE YOU WATCH **Circle the words you hear.** Watch scene 4.1.

| baby | camera | captivity | costume | forest |
|---|---|---|---|---|
| leopard | mother | mountain | school | student |

A giant panda cub, Wolong, Sichuan Province, China

**4** AFTER YOU WATCH **Work in pairs.** Tick T for *True* or F for *False*.

1. China takes pandas born in captivity and releases them into the wild. T F
2. Mother pandas go for several months without food and water after their baby is born. T F
3. Baby pandas grow very slowly. T F
4. 'Papa Panda' is the name of a very old panda at the Wolong China Conservation and Research Centre. T F
5. Workers at the Conservation Centre teach pandas how to live in the wild. T F
6. Leopards and pandas often play together at the Conservation Centre. T F

**5** **Work in pairs.** At the beginning of the video, Ami says, 'As a National Geographic photographer, my job is to surprise people'. Which photos or facts in the video surprised you? Explain.

**6** **Work in groups.** In the video, workers try to prepare pandas for life in the wild. Think about how animals survive in the wild. What do they need to do and know in order to survive? Make a list of the most important skills.

**7** YOU DECIDE **Choose an activity.**

1. **Work independently.** What do you want to know about the life of a worker at the Wolong China Conservation and Research Centre? Write a list of questions. Then read your questions to the class and ask them to suggest possible answers.
2. **Work in pairs.** Role-play a conversation between Ami and a reporter who wants to know about her experiences in China. Share your dialogue with the class.
3. **Work in groups.** Find out about an endangered animal and ways to protect it. Share with the class.

## GRAMMAR 077

**Adverbs: Saying how you do something**

Cheetahs are fast runners. They can run very **fast** at 113 kilometres per hour.

Elephants are good at swimming. They can swim very **well**.

The three-toed sloth is a slow animal. It moves very **slowly**.

The howler monkey has got a loud voice. It can call very **loudly**.

good → well    high → high    easy → easily

fast → fast    bad → badly    gentle → gently

**1** **Work in pairs.** Complete the sentences with the correct form of a word from the box.

| bad | easy | good | high | loud | fast | quiet |
|---|---|---|---|---|---|---|

Cats can jump very ______________. They can jump five times their own height. They can run very ______________ at 50 kilometres per hour. They have got good noses, and they can smell things very ______________ from far away. They have also got very good ears. Even if you speak ______________, your cat can hear you! All cats meow when they are angry or hungry, but some cats are very noisy. Siamese cats are famous because they meow ______________ when they are hungry. Cats are also good at climbing. It isn't difficult for them to climb trees. They can go up very ______________, but sometimes they forget how to come down again!

**2** **Work in pairs.** Make sentences about the animals below and their abilities.

| dogs | dolphins | pandas | parrots | snakes | tigers |
|---|---|---|---|---|---|
| climb | hear | move | run | speak | swim |
| easily | fast | loudly | quickly | quietly | well |

**3** **Work in pairs.** Play *Noughts and Crosses*. Make adverbs from the words in the grid. Use them to describe things that you can or can't do. Mark X or O. Try to get three in a row.

| good | bad | fast |
|---|---|---|
| loud | quiet | slow |
| easy | high | quick |

I can't swim very well!

## WRITING

When we write a fact sheet, we need to check all the facts carefully.

Separate the facts into different sections. We can separate the facts with headings or bullet points:

***Diet***

*Parrots eat fruit, seeds and small insects.*

***Habitat***

*A lot of parrots live in the rain forest.*

***Fun facts***

- *Parrots are often brightly coloured.*
- *There are more than 350 different types of parrot.*

1 **Read the model.** How does the writer separate the information? Underline the headings and circle the bullet points.

### The Capybara

The capybara is a large hairy mammal. It's the size of a pig – about 50–60 centimetres tall and about 100–130 centimetres long. It weighs between 30 and 80 kilograms. It hasn't got a tail.

**Habitat:**

Capybaras are from South and Central America. They always live near water.

**Diet:**

Capybaras are herbivores. They eat water plants and grass. They don't eat meat.

**Fun facts:**

- Capybaras can swim very well. They can stay under the water for five minutes.
- Capybaras are very friendly. They usually live together in large groups.
- Capybaras are very noisy! They can make a lot of different sounds.

2 **Work in pairs.** Look at the questions about capybaras. Which ones can you answer using information from the fact sheet?

- What do they eat?
- How big are they?
- Where do they live?
- How fast can they run?
- How much do they eat?
- Do they live alone or in groups?

3 **Write.** Write a fact sheet about a different animal. Choose an animal from this unit or any other animal. Use headings and bullet points to separate the facts.

Four squirrel monkeys on a capybara

# Use Your Skills

**'Do whatever is in your reach … we need to act, and act now.'**

**Juliana Machado Ferreira**
**National Geographic Explorer, Conservation Biologist**

1. **Watch scene 4.2.**
2. Juliana talks about doing 'whatever is in your reach'. Think about Juliana's work. How does she use her special knowledge and abilities to help animals?
3. Think about some problems in your own area. How can you use your knowledge and abilities to help solve these problems?

# Make an Impact

**YOU DECIDE** **Choose a project.**

**1 Plan and hold an endangered animal quiz.**

- Prepare cards with *true* or *false* sentences about endangered animals.
- Organise two teams in your class.
- Hold the quiz. Read each fact aloud. Classmates say if your sentence is true or false.

**2 Write a diary entry.**

- Imagine that you work at a wildlife reserve. Think about which animals you look after and what you do.
- Write a description of your day. Include photos.
- Show your diary entry to your classmates. Answer their questions about it.

**3 Make a wild animal poster.**

- Choose a wild animal and find out about it. Collect information and photos.
- Organise your information on a poster.
- Display your poster in the classroom. Present it to your classmates.

Golden snub-nosed monkeys

# Express Yourself

**1** **Read and listen to the advertisement.** 078

# Robotosaurus Rex

**This amazing remote-controlled robot dinosaur is more than a toy –**

## IT'S A PET AND A FRIEND!

- Clap your hands to make your dinosaur sit or stand.
- Use the remote control to make your dinosaur walk, run fast or lie down.
- Play music through the remote control to make your dinosaur dance!
- Throw the remote control and watch your dinosaur chase it.
- Look at the lights on your dinosaur's back to check its mood:

| BLUE | RED | GREEN | YELLOW |
| --- | --- | --- | --- |
| happy | angry | tired | hungry |

Remote control

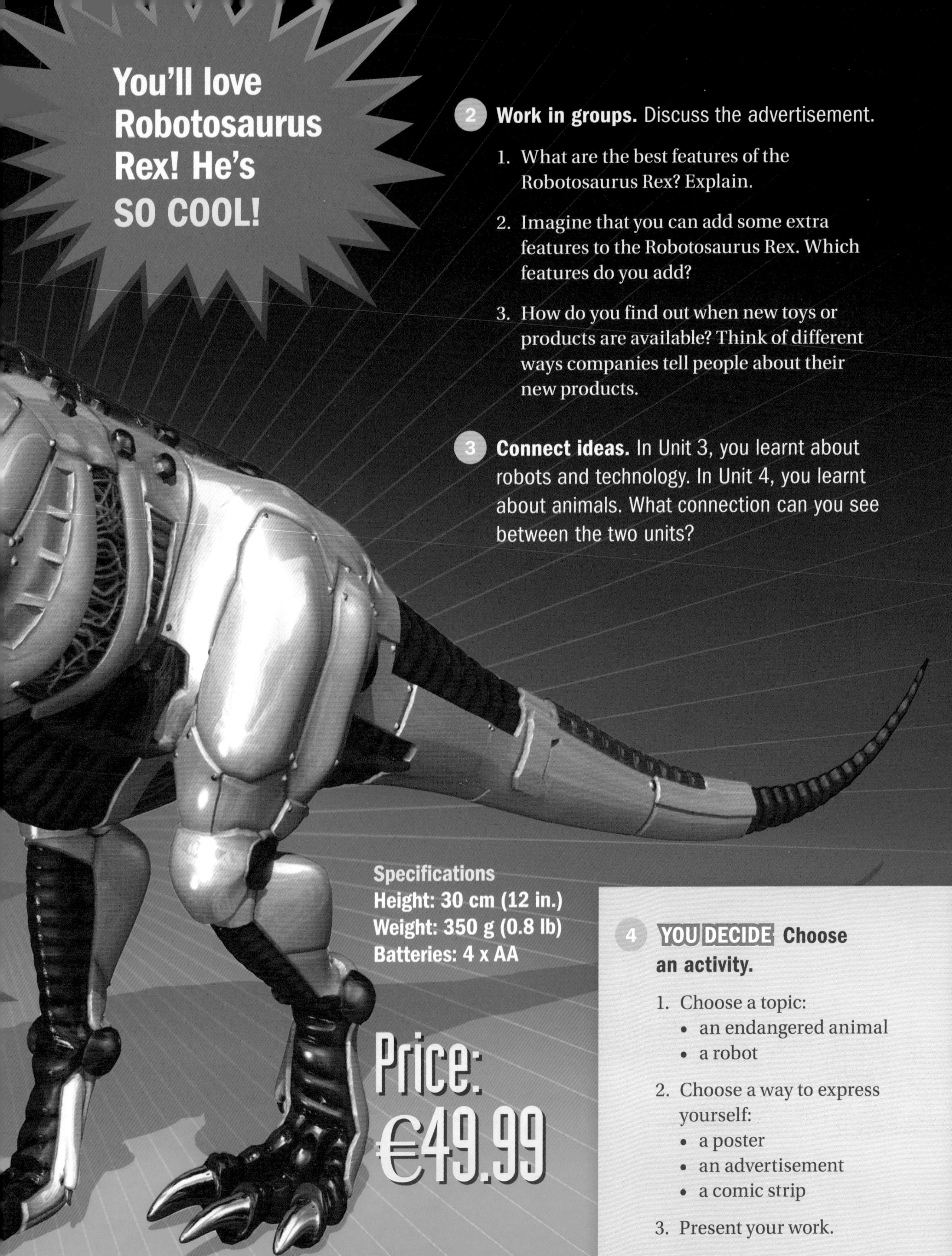


2 **Work in groups.** Discuss the advertisement.

1. What are the best features of the Robotosaurus Rex? Explain.
2. Imagine that you can add some extra features to the Robotosaurus Rex. Which features do you add?
3. How do you find out when new toys or products are available? Think of different ways companies tell people about their new products.

3 **Connect ideas.** In Unit 3, you learnt about robots and technology. In Unit 4, you learnt about animals. What connection can you see between the two units?

4 **YOU DECIDE Choose an activity.**

1. Choose a topic:
   - an endangered animal
   - a robot
2. Choose a way to express yourself:
   - a poster
   - an advertisement
   - a comic strip
3. Present your work.

Unit 5

# Water

The Colorado River Delta, from 300 metres above

**'Rivers affect the health of our seas, wildlife, communities and economies.'**
**Osvel Hinojosa Huerta**

## TO START

1. Look at the photo. What do you see?
2. Think about how you use water at home. What do you use it for? How often do you use it?
3. Osvel Hinojosa Huerta talks about the importance of rivers. Do you live near any rivers? How do people use them? Give examples.

**1 Where does your water come from?**
Discuss. Then listen and read. 079

You turn on a tap and water comes out of it. But do you know where your water comes from? Earth is sometimes called 'The Blue Planet' because 71 per cent of its surface is covered in water. This water is in a continuous cycle. It is always moving on, above and below the surface of the earth. Let's look at the water cycle.

### WATER GIVES LIFE, BUT IT IS ALSO A KILLER!

Less than 1% of the water on Earth is fresh water, and not all of that water is clean and safe to drink.

- Unsafe water is one of the top ten killers in the world.
- Dirty water causes 80% of all diseases in some parts of the world.

There is snow on the mountains. Some snow turns into **ice**.

Sometimes the ice and snow on the mountains **melts**. Then it runs onto the **ground** and down the side of the mountains.

Some of the water goes **underground**. Some water flows from the ground into **oceans**, **lakes** and **rivers**.

2 **LEARN NEW WORDS Listen and repeat.** 080

3 **Work in pairs.** Talk about why the water cycle is important to us.

## 4 Read and write the words from the list.

**cloud** **fresh water** **ground** **ocean** **rain** **river** **salt water** **sky**

The Colorado ________________ is 2,330 km (1,448 mi) long. It flows from the Rocky Mountains in the USA, through five states and into Mexico. It finally flows out into the Delta wetlands. The ________________ in the wetlands is very important for wildlife and plants. From the wetlands, the river then joins the ________________ of the ________________ in the Gulf of California. But there is a problem. Factories, farms and cities are using a lot of water from the Delta wetlands. There is also less ________________ than there was in the past. This means that the ________________ in some parts is now completely dry. Osvel Hinojosa Huerta is a National Geographic conservationist. He is working together with businesses, farmers and industries to save the Delta wetlands. He wants to put water back into the wetlands.

Sandra Postel and Osvel Hinojosa Huerta

## 5 LEARN NEW WORDS Listen to these words and match them to their definitions. Then listen and repeat. 081 082

**clean** **dirty** **safe** **unsafe**

________________ 1. not safe, dangerous

________________ 2. free from dirt or marks

________________ 3. not dangerous

________________ 4. covered with dirt or marks

## 6 YOU DECIDE Choose an activity.

1. **Work independently.** Find different bodies of water near where you live. Look for rivers, lakes or ponds. Draw and label a map to show where they are.
2. **Work in pairs.** How much water do you use in your daily life? Talk about an average day, and make a list of every time you use water.
3. **Work in groups.** Research groups that help people find clean, safe water. Learn about where they work and what they do. Share what you learn with the class.

## SPEAKING STRATEGY 083

**Brainstorming solutions**

**How can** we save water?

**What about** young people? What can they do?

**What can** we do in the garden to save water?

**Have you got** any other ideas?

**Maybe** we can have shorter showers?

**What if** they learn about the water cycle at school?

**I think we should** collect rainwater for the plants.

**Sorry**, I can't think of anything.

**1 Listen.** How do the speakers brainstorm solutions? Write the phrases you hear. 084

LET'S SAVE THE WATER TOGETHER

**2 Read and complete the dialogue.**

Stefan: ______________ we do at school to save water?

Frieda: At school? ______________ put some posters up in the toilets about saving water. Then people will remember to turn the taps off.

Stefan: Good idea. ______________ teachers? What can they do?

Frieda: ______________ they show us some videos about saving water and ask us to research other ways?

Stefan: Yes, OK. And ______________ we save water in the school kitchen?

Frieda: Sorry, I can't think of anything.

Stefan: OK, never mind. ______________ any other ideas?

Frieda: Yes. ______________ plant more trees in the school garden. Trees don't need so much water.

Stefan: Great idea. Thanks, Frieda.

**3 Work in pairs.** Take turns. Choose a card. Brainstorm solutions.

**Go to page 179.**

## GRAMMAR 085

**Present continuous: Talking about what is happening now**

How **are we trying** to save water?

People **aren't running** the tap for a long time to get cold water. **They're keeping** water cold in the fridge.

Apps **are helping** people to save water in the garden.

**Talking about things that always happen**

My brother **is always having** long showers!

Our neighbour **is always washing** his car with a lot of water.

**1 Listen.** You will hear about six ways that people are trying to save water. Number the words in the order you hear them. Then write them out in the correct form. 086

_____ buy My parents are buying _____

_____ put We _____

_____ help We _____

_____ keep I _____

_____ plant I _____

_____ talk My sister _____

**2 Read.** Complete the text with the correct form of the verb in brackets.

What _____ (you / do) today?

We're on Day One of our Water Saving Plan at home. Mum and Dad _____ (try) really hard to save water at the moment, but Hugo, my little brother, _____ (not help) us at all. He _____ (always play) with the hose in the garden, and his friends _____ (always turn) on the tap in the kitchen and then running away. We _____ (get) very annoyed with them! Have you got any advice for us?

**3** **LEARN NEW WORDS Listen to learn about other ways of saving water.** Then listen and repeat. 087 088

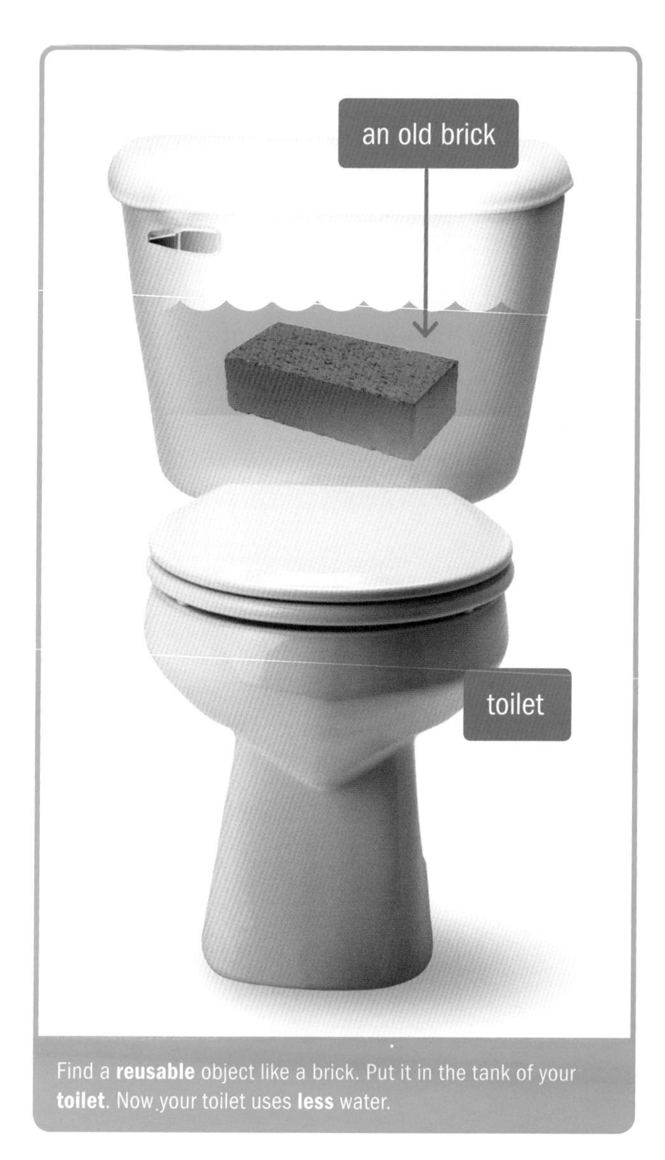


Find a **reusable** object like a brick. Put it in the tank of your **toilet**. Now your toilet uses **less** water.

Collect the water from your roof. Water runs through your gutter and a special container collects it. Now you can **water** your garden!

**4** **Work independently.** Imagine that you are trying to save water at home. Write a list of the things you're doing to help. Use words from the box.

| | | | | |
|---|---|---|---|---|
| **garden** | **less** | **plants** | **reusable** | **shower** |
| **tap** | **toilet** | **wash** | **water** | |

**5** **Work in pairs.** Compare your lists from Activity 4. Do you have similar ideas?

1 **BEFORE YOU READ Discuss in pairs.** Look at the title and the photo. What do you think the reading is about?

2 **LEARN NEW WORDS Find these words in the reading.** Which two words are types of material? Which two words mean to do something again? Then listen and repeat. 089

| **cloth** | **plastic** | **recycle** | **re-use** |
|---|---|---|---|

3 **WHILE YOU READ Look for examples and explanations.** 090

# Keep our oceans clean!

Look around you. Do you see anything made with plastic? We use plastic in our computers, in our phones, in our homes, in our cars and even in our clothes!

We make 300 million tonnes of plastic every year. That's about the same weight as 30 million adult elephants! Plastic is very useful, but there's a problem. When we don't want things made of plastic anymore, we often throw them away.

# An Ocean of Plastic

A lot of that plastic ends up in our oceans. In fact, every year, at least 8 million tonnes of plastic goes into our oceans. This plastic breaks up into very small pieces called microplastics. Sea animals and fish eat the microplastics and may die.

Microplastics are not the only problem. Tiny pieces of plastic, called microbeads, are added to many types of toothpaste and shampoo. When we use these products, the microbeads go into the water and fish eat them. However, because microbeads are not food and are not nutritious, the fish then die. Microbeads can also pass into our systems when we eat fish.

There are things we can do to stop plastic reaching the ocean. Some countries have now banned the use of microbeads in products. We can also reduce the amount of plastic we use and find ways to recycle it. Don't use plastic bags. When you go shopping, take cloth bags to the shop with you and re-use them. Recycle your plastic bottles at home and at school. If you live near a beach, join or start a clean-up group. Let's all work together to keep our oceans clean!

**A grey triggerfish below rubbish floating in the Atlantic Ocean, Palm Beach, Florida**

**4** AFTER YOU READ **Work in pairs to answer the questions.**

1. How much plastic do we make every year?
2. What do we sometimes do when we don't want our plastic?
3. What happens to plastic when it goes into our oceans?
4. What happens when fish eat microplastics?
5. What kinds of products have microbeads in them?
6. Why are cloth bags better than plastic bags?

**5** **Work in pairs.** How does the author give examples or explanations to answer these questions? Underline the sentences.

1. 300 million tonnes of plastic is the same weight as how many elephants?
2. What happens when we use products with microbeads?
3. Give an example of how people can re-use or recycle plastic.

**6** **Discuss in groups.**

1. Does the reading change the way you feel about plastic? Why or why not?
2. How much plastic is in your classroom? Make a list of all the plastic things you can see. Compare your list with other groups.
3. What happens when fish and sea animals die because of plastic in the oceans? How can this affect other animals or humans?

# VIDEO

**1** BEFORE YOU WATCH **Discuss in pairs.**

1. How often do you go swimming? Where do you go swimming?
2. Do you ever find plastic bags or other litter in the water? How do you feel when you find litter in the water?

**2** **Work in pairs.** You are going to watch *Boyan's Big Idea*. Before you watch, look at the photo of Boyan's invention. What do you think his big idea is?

**3** WHILE YOU WATCH **Check your prediction from Activity 2.** Watch scene 9.1.

**4** AFTER YOU WATCH **Work in pairs to answer these questions.**

1. How old is Boyan in 2010?
2. What do he and his friend see when they are diving in Greece?
3. How many tonnes of plastic go into the ocean every year?
4. What happens to the trash after it collects at the centre of Boyan's invention?
5. When does Boyan put a model of his invention into the North Sea?
6. When does Boyan want to put his invention into the Pacific Ocean?

5 **Work in groups.** What do you think about Boyan's idea? Discuss any possible problems.

6 **Work in pairs.** Plastic isn't the only problem in our ocean. What other environmental problems are there? Discuss your ideas together.

The Ocean Cleanup North Sea Prototype in The Hague, Netherlands

7 **YOU DECIDE** **Choose an activity.**

1. **Work independently.** Find out about ways you can help to reduce plastic pollution. Make a list of your ideas.
2. **Work in pairs.** Design a poster to tell people not to use plastic bags. Include some information about plastic in the oceans.
3. **Work in groups.** Create an advertisement for Boyan's Ocean Cleanup system. Use music and images. Act it out for the class or make a video.

## GRAMMAR 091

***There was* and *There were*: Talking about the past**

**The Han River, South Korea**

| **In the 1970s ...** | **Now ...** |
|---|---|
| **There was** pollution in the water. | There isn't any pollution in the water. |
| **There were** a lot of dead fish in the river. | There aren't any dead fish in the river. |
| **There wasn't** any food for the wildlife. | There is plenty of food for the wildlife. |
| **There weren't** any birds near the water. | There are many types of birds in and near the water. |

**1** **Read.** Complete the paragraph with *there was*, *there were*, *there wasn't* or *there weren't*.

In the 1950s and 1960s, in Singapore, ________________ a big problem with the Singapore River. ________________ a lot of rubbish in the water. ________________ farms and factories very close to the river, and ________________ a lot of pollution from these places. ________________ many tourists near the river because it was dirty. ________________ any clean water in the river. Then, in 1977, ________________ a big clean-up project. Now the Singapore River is clean and beautiful. Many tourists come to visit the parks and museums near the river.

The Singapore River in the 1960s

The Singapore River, 2016

**2** **Work in pairs.** Throw a coin and move ahead. (Heads = 1 space; tails = 2 spaces.) When you land on a space, make a sentence about how the park was in the past and how it is now.

In the past there was rubbish on the grass, but now there's no rubbish on the grass.

Go to page 183.

## WRITING

In persuasive writing, we try to make the reader think or do something. We can give advice with phrases like:

> ***It's really important to*** *save water.*
> ***It's a good idea to*** *have a quick shower instead of a bath.*
> ***You should*** *use a reusable water bottle.*
> ***You shouldn't*** *leave the tap on.*

1 **Read the model.** Work in pairs to identify and underline the phrases that persuade the reader.

**Save Water!**

Water is very important. We drink it, we wash in it, we swim in it and we cook with it. It's really important to save water at school. How can you help? In the classroom, you should use reusable water bottles. In the toilets, you should remember to turn off the tap after you wash your hands. Teachers can also help. They should teach us about the water cycle at school. We should have posters about water in our classrooms. It's a good idea to collect rainwater in a special container and use it to water the trees and plants in the school garden. Remember – save water at school!

2 **Work in pairs.** Do you already do things to save water at your school? What do you do?

3 **Write.** Write a paragraph to persuade people to save water at home. Include some ideas from pages 99 and 101.

# Protect Our Water

**'We turn on our tap, but we don't know where the water comes from.'**

**Osvel Hinojosa Huerta**
**National Geographic Explorer, Conservationist**

1. **Watch scene 5.2.**
2. Read Osvel's quote. Do you know where your water comes from? How can knowing where your water comes from change the way you use water every day?
3. Choose a local lake or river. Find out about the plants and wildlife there. How can you help to protect this place or to clean it up?

# Make an Impact

**YOU DECIDE** **Choose a project.**

### 1 Make a clean-up day poster.

- Imagine that a local park, river or lake is holding a clean-up day.
- Create a poster to advertise the day. Include information about why the clean-up project is important.
- Display your poster in the classroom. Talk to your classmates about the day and answer their questions.

### 2 Create a comic strip.

- Think of a short story about rubbish in a river.
- Design a comic strip to illustrate the story.
- Share your comic strip with the class.

### 3 Give a presentation.

- Find information about different ways that a city can save water.
- Make a list of the most useful advice and find pictures to illustrate your ideas.
- Present your advice to the class.

Volunteers from a school collect rubbish from Manila Bay, Philippines

Unit 6

# The City
## Past, Present and Future

'The structures, the art and the buildings that we build during our lifetime are our way of communicating with the people around us and with future generations.'
**Ross Davison**

Moscow, Russia, at night

## TO START

1. Look at the photo. What do you see? Do you want to live in a city like this? Why or why not?
2. Ross Davison thinks that we can communicate with future generations through our buildings. Think about a famous building or structure. What message does it communicate to you?
3. Think about a place in your area that you love. Why do you like it? Which things about that place are most important?

1 **What buildings do you like to look at?** Discuss. Then listen and read. 092

A five-storey house and garden in Tokyo, Japan

Iwan Baan is an architectural photographer. He travels 52 weeks of the year, taking photos of **buildings** and the people who live in them. Sometimes he takes photos of buildings because they bring nature into the city, such as the tiny five-storey garden building in the **centre** of Tokyo, Japan. Sometimes he takes photos of buildings because they are very beautiful, such as Zaha Hadid's **amazing** MAXXI **museum** in Rome.

He also takes photos of buildings such as the Butaro **hospital** in Burera, Rwanda, because they are **important** and they help the community. Before this hospital opened in Burera in 2011, there were no doctors in this whole district of 340,000 people.

Some buildings have more than one **focus**, like the Tenerife Espacio de las Artes (TEA), a cultural centre in Spain. Iwan took photos of this **interesting** building in 2009. The TEA is a library, art museum, shop and restaurant in one! It brings together people of all ages and interests. It's a very **busy** place. But don't worry about queuing up to get in. The building has an **entrance** on every side! The inside of the TEA has many beautiful galleries, but there's no roof at the centre of the building – it's an outdoor space shaped like a triangle. There, you can sit outside and eat a snack during the day or watch a film at night.

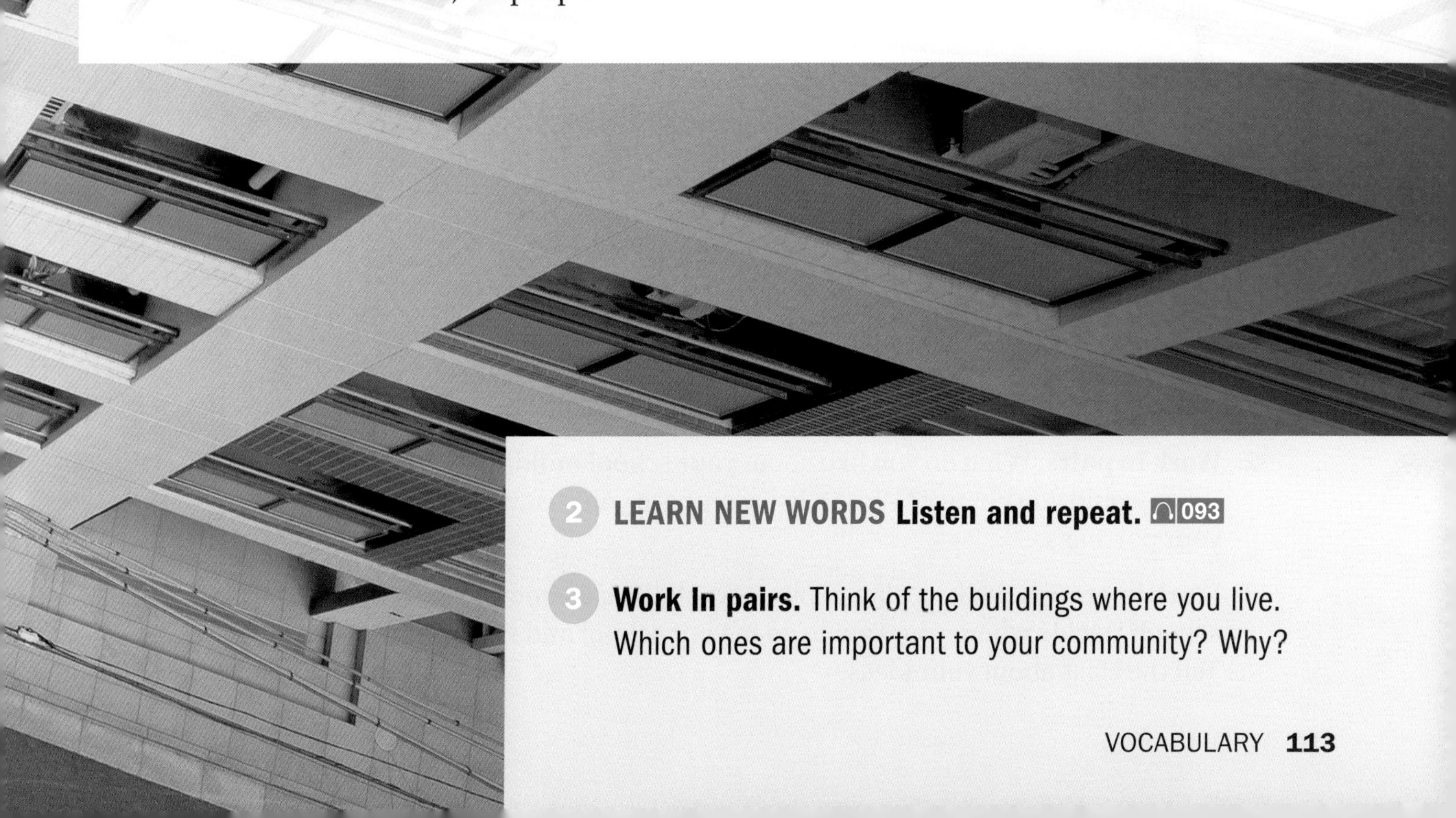

2 **LEARN NEW WORDS Listen and repeat.** 093

3 **Work in pairs.** Think of the buildings where you live. Which ones are important to your community? Why?

## 4 Read and write the words from the list.

| amazing | buildings | centre | entrance | focus | hospital | important | museum |
|---|---|---|---|---|---|---|---|

Ross Davison works for CyArk, an organisation that keeps online images of important cultural places. He travels to places around the world. These places are ________________ because the ________________ there are very old, and they can tell us a lot about how people lived in the past. Ross uses CyArk's special cameras to make images of these ________________ places before they disappear forever. For example, in Syria, Ross and his team made a 3D image of a 13th-century ________________ in the ________________ of Damascus. In the past, this was a place for sick people, but now it is an important historical site. Ross also teaches local people to use CyArk's special cameras. In Beirut, Ross used the Sursock ________________ as his classroom. The local team used CyArk's cameras on the historical objects there.

Ross Davison working with CyArk

## 5 LEARN NEW WORDS Listen to these words and use them to complete the sentences. Then listen and repeat. 094 095

| inside | outside | roof | take photos |
|---|---|---|---|

1. Ross Davison uses special cameras to ________________ of important buildings.
2. From the ________________, this building doesn't look very interesting.
3. When you go ________________ the building, you see that it's a beautiful home.
4. This building even has a tennis court on the ________________!

## 6 YOU DECIDE Choose an activity.

1. **Work independently.** Imagine a house that you would want to live in. What would it be like? Write a short description.
2. **Work in pairs.** What do you like about your school building? What would you change? Write a list. Compare your list with your partner's.
3. **Work in groups.** Make a plan to photograph the classrooms and students in your school. Decide where you want to go in your school and what photos you want to take. Tell the class about your ideas.

## SPEAKING STRATEGY 096

**Expressing opinions and responding to them**

**I love** photos of empty buildings.

**I think that** this building is beautiful.

**I don't like** the buildings in this street.

**I think** it's important to keep a record of our historic sites.

**I don't. I prefer** photos with people in them.

**I don't agree.** / **No way**! I don't like it at all.

**Me neither!** I think they're really boring.

**Me too!** / **Absolutely!** They're really important.

The Maracanã Stadium, Rio de Janeiro, Brazil

1 **Listen.** How do the speakers agree and disagree? Write the phrases you hear. 097

2 **Read and complete the dialogue.**

Livia: ______________ these Iwan Baan photos of the CCTV building in China. ______________ they're amazing!

Bruno: ______________! They are really interesting. But ______________ his photos of Zaha Hadid's MAXXI building in Rome. ______________ looking at photos of buildings without people.

Livia: ______________! People make the photos more interesting. Empty buildings are boring.

Bruno: ______________. I want to look at the architecture – the walls, the floor and the roof – not the people.

3 **Work in pairs.** Choose a card. Read the sentence. Give your opinion. Your partner will then agree or disagree.

'Museums are interesting places.' Yes, I think museums are interesting places. I like art museums.

I don't agree. I think museums are really boring!

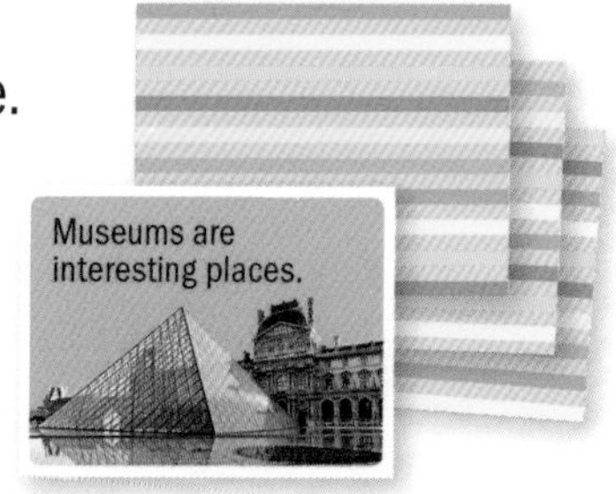


**Go to page 185.**

## GRAMMAR 098

**Past simple: Talking about the past**

In July 2016, Ross and his team **visited** Naxos island in Greece.
They **took** photos of a temple, a church and a castle there.
They **carried** all their equipment in rucksacks on their backs.
They **loved** seeing the ancient buildings.

visit → visited
love → loved
carry → carried

take → took
go → went
build → built

1 **Listen.** You will hear about a CyArk project in Hawaii. Circle the past simple verbs you hear. 099

| came | created | learnt | made | sent | started |
|---|---|---|---|---|---|
| studied | thought | took | visited | wanted | worked |

2 **Read.** Complete the text with the past simple form of the verb in brackets.

In January 2015, Ross Davison ________ (visit) a high school in Armenia. He ________ (work) with an advanced after-school club of 21 students. They ________ (go) to a famous monastery near the school. They ________ (use) cameras and special equipment to take scans of the site. Then they ________ (return) to the school. They ________ (create) 3D models and animations of the site from their photos. The project ________ (take) a week. After the students ________ (finish) the project, they ________ (give) a presentation at their school. Two hundred students, teachers and parents ________ (come) to the presentation.

3 **LEARN NEW WORDS Listen to learn about some amazing buildings.** Then listen and repeat. 100 101

The amphitheatre in Cartagena, Spain, is a Roman open-air **theatre**.

The **Cathedral** of Brasilia in Brazil is a very modern building.

Himeji **Castle** in Japan looks like a white bird.

The Sheikh Zayed **Mosque** in the United Arab Emirates has enough space for more than 40,000 people.

4 **Work in pairs.** Listen again. Circle the correct words. 102

1. More than two million people *visit / visited* Himeji *Cathedral / Castle* in 2015.
2. Sheikh Zayed *Castle / Mosque* in the United Arab Emirates *open / opened* in 2007.
3. I *went / go* to the *Cathedral / Theatre* of Brasilia with my grandparents last year.
4. Last week, 7,000 people *watched / watch* plays and races at the open-air *mosque / theatre* in Cartagena.

5 **Work independently.** Imagine you visited one of the places above. Write a postcard about your visit. Describe how you got there, what you saw and what you did.

1 BEFORE YOU READ **Discuss in pairs.** Look at the title and the photo. What do you think the reading is about?

2 LEARN NEW WORDS **Find these words in the reading.** What do you think they mean? Which four words would you find in a maths lesson? Then listen and repeat. 103

| angle | curve | rectangle | straight line | unusual |
|---|---|---|---|---|

3 WHILE YOU READ **Think about why the author wrote this text.** 104

4 AFTER YOU READ **Work in pairs to answer the questions.**

1. Why did no one want to build Zaha Hadid's buildings in her early career?
2. Name four countries where Zaha Hadid lived.
3. Give three reasons why, according to Zaha Hadid, people had problems with her.
4. What can you find in the MAXXI museum in Rome?
5. Are Zaha Hadid's buildings popular with everyone? Find a sentence in the text to support your answer.

5 **Work in pairs.** Why did the author write this text? Tick the best reason. Explain your choice.

____ to write a short biography of Zaha Hadid's life

____ to express his/her opinion about Zaha Hadid's work

____ to persuade the reader to visit some of Zaha Hadid's buildings

6 **Discuss in groups.**

1. Zaha Hadid said, 'We don't make nice little buildings. ... The world is not a rectangle.' What do you think she means? Can you think of examples of 'nice little buildings' in your area?
2. Imagine that you can design a new public building for your city or town. What type of building do you design and why? Do you use an old or new style of architecture for your building?
3. What different things do architects have to think about when they design a building? Discuss your ideas and make a list.

Guangzhou Opera House, Guangzhou, China

# Queen OF THE Curve

## Zaha Hadid: the architect who didn't build *nice* buildings

Zaha Hadid (1950–2016) was one of the most famous architects in the world. She was called 'Queen of the Curve' because her buildings often had huge curves, as well as straight lines and sharp angles. But she wasn't always successful. At the beginning of her career, architecture magazines published her amazing drawings of buildings, but no one wanted to build them! Her ideas were too unusual and often very expensive.

Zaha Hadid was born in Baghdad, Iraq. She went to school in Switzerland and England and then studied maths at university in Beirut, Lebanon. In 1972, she moved to London, England, to study architecture. Life wasn't always easy for her. 'I'm a woman and that's a problem for some people,' she explained once. 'I'm a foreigner, and I do work which is *not normative* (unusual).'

Today, there are 40 Zaha Hadid buildings and structures around the world. You can listen to opera at the Guangzhou Opera House in the city of Guangzhou, China. You can cross the Sheikh Zayed Bridge in Abu Dhabi. You can go swimming at the Aquatics Centre in London, England, and you can look at 21st-century art at the MAXXI museum in Rome, Italy. In all of these places, you can see the shapes, curves and angles of Hadid's structures. Hadid's work is exciting, interesting and unusual. Not everyone likes it, but it's never boring. 'We don't make nice little buildings,' she said in a newspaper interview in 2013. 'The world is not a rectangle.'

# VIDEO

1 BEFORE YOU WATCH **Discuss in pairs.** Look at the photo. Discuss the questions below.

1. What do you think happened to this temple?
2. Do you think people can rebuild it? How?
3. Can they find out exactly how it looked in the past? How?

2 **Work in pairs.** You are going to watch *Preserving Our Heritage with Ross Davison.* From the title, predict what the video is about. Circle the letter.

a. Using images to keep information about important buildings

b. Using buildings to find out about the past

3 WHILE YOU WATCH **Check your prediction from Activity 2.** **Watch scene 6.1.**

**A temple in Bagan, Myanmar, the day after a powerful earthquake**

4 AFTER YOU WATCH **Work in pairs to put these events in the correct order.**

a. ____ Ross makes a digital model of the building.

b. ____ Ross studies the site.

c. ____ Ross uses flying cameras to take pictures of the landscape.

d. ____ Ross uses special cameras to take 3D images.

5 **Work in pairs to answer the questions.**

1. When did Ross first visit Bagan?
2. What happened a few months after Ross's trip?
3. How did Ross's photos of the building in Bagan help solve the problem?
4. What does Ross teach his students?
5. What does the student from Lahore think about Ross?

6 **Work in pairs.** In the video, Ross explains that our heritage is our personal history and buildings are part of that history. What other things make up our heritage? Make a list of your ideas.

7 **Work in groups.** Earthquakes are just one possible problem for historic buildings. What other problems are there? How can we protect our buildings in the future? Discuss your ideas together.

8 YOU DECIDE **Choose an activity.**

1. **Work independently.** Find out about another historic building that was damaged in an earthquake or another disaster. What happened to it? Write a short report about it.
2. **Work in pairs.** Ross sometimes visits schools. He talks to students about historic buildings and teaches them to use his equipment. Write a letter to Ross, inviting him to visit your school. Explain why you want him to come.
3. **Work in groups.** Imagine that you can work with Ross to make a 3D image of one building in your city or town. Which building will you choose? Why?

## GRAMMAR 105

**Past simple: Asking questions about the past**

Where **did** you **go** last summer?

We **went** to Beijing. We **didn't fly** there. We **went** by train.

**Did** you **visit** the National Centre for the Performing Arts?

Yes, we **did**. We **didn't see** a performance there, but we **looked** at the building.

1 **Read.** Complete the dialogue with the correct past simple form of the verb in brackets.

Nico: Hi, Florence. ____________________ (enjoy) your trip to Spain last month?

Florence: Yes, we ____________________ (do), thank you! It was a great trip.

Nico: Where ____________________ (you / go)?

Florence: We went to Barcelona and Bilbao.

Nico: ____________________ (you / visit) the Guggenheim Museum in Bilbao?

Florence: Yes, we did. I loved it, but my brother ____________________ (not / like) it at all! He hates modern architecture.

Nico: Really? No way! ____________________ (you / look) at the modern art inside?

Florence: No, we didn't. We ____________________ (not / have) enough time. We were only in Bilbao for one day, and then we went to Barcelona.

Nico: How long ____________________ (you / spend) in Barcelona?

Florence: Four days. It was amazing! My favourite building was the Sagrada Familia Cathedral. I ____________________ (not / want) to come home!

2 **Work in pairs.** Take turns throwing the cube. Use the words on the cube to make a past simple question. Answer your partner's questions.

**Go to page 175.**

## WRITING

When we write a paragraph of opinion, we present several reasons to support our argument. The following words can help you to introduce your reasons:

**firstly** **secondly** **finally**

1 **Read the model.** Work in pairs to identify and underline the examples that support the writer's opinion.

### Sagrada Familia

There are many beautiful buildings in Barcelona, but my favourite building is the Sagrada Familia. The architect, Antoni Gaudí, started to build this amazing church in 1882, and it still isn't completed today! Although it isn't completed, it's still important for several reasons. Firstly, it's a very tall church. You can see it from very far away because it is 170 m (560 ft) tall. Secondly, it looks very unusual. Not everyone likes it, but people always enjoy talking about it. Some people think it looks like a forest made of stone. Other people think it looks like a house from a fairy tale. Finally, Gaudí used the natural world for his design. He thought about mountains, trees and rocks when he designed this building. For these reasons, I think the Sagrada Familia is a very important and amazing building.

2 **Work in pairs.** Find and circle the adjectives that the writer uses to describe the Sagrada Familia.

3 **Write.** Write about your favourite building or structure. Explain why it is your favourite. Give three reasons that support your opinion.

# Know Your History

**'You are the guardians of your local history. This is your culture.'**

**Ross Davison**
**National Geographic Explorer, Heritage Conservationist**

1. **Watch scene 6.2.**
2. Ross Davison says that we are the guardians of our local history. A *guardian* is a person who preserves and protects something. How can we preserve our own culture for the next generation?
3. What is your culture? Describe the people, places, things and actions that make up your culture.

# Make an Impact

**YOU DECIDE** **Choose a project.**

## 1 Plan and create an architecture display.

- Work as a group to prepare a list of buildings in your area that are interesting, unusual or historically important.
- Find or take photos and write sentences about each building.
- Create a display with your photos and sentences. Share it with the class.

## 2 Make a biographical poster.

- Research an architect who designed some unusual buildings or buildings that you really like.
- Prepare a biography of that person. Include photos of some of their buildings.
- Create a poster and share the information with the class.

## 3 Design a new school building.

- Think of a design for your school building. It should look good and be practical.
- Draw a picture of your design. Use curves, angles and straight lines to make it interesting.
- Present your design to the class and answer their questions about it.

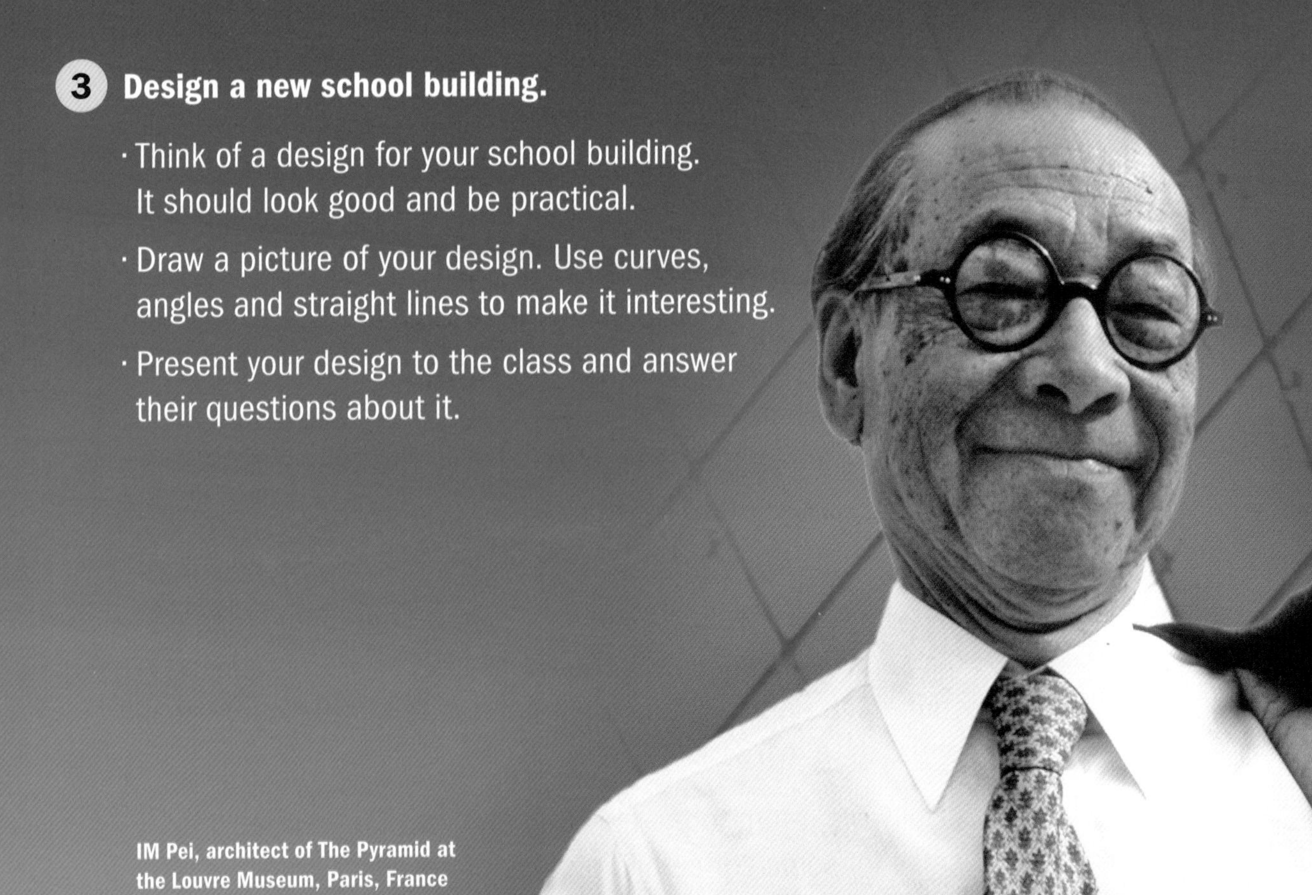

**IM Pei, architect of The Pyramid at the Louvre Museum, Paris, France**

# Express Yourself

1 **Read and listen to the tour description.** 106

## A TOUR OF Thun, Switzerland

Welcome to Thun, Switzerland – a beautiful town by the River Aare, at the west end of Lake Thun.

Join us on a three-hour tour of the town and discover some of Thun's amazing buildings and sights.

We begin our tour at the bus station. Next, we cross a bridge over the River Aare to the island of Bälliz. This is Thun's shopping area. There are a lot of expensive clothing stores here, but you can also buy fruit, vegetables and flowers on Wednesdays and Saturdays at the market.

Next, we cross another bridge to visit Castle Thun in the old town. The castle is more than 800 years old. It is now a museum and concert hall. After we visit the castle, it's time for lunch! If the weather is sunny, we can eat at one of the outdoor cafés by the river.

After lunch, we walk to Schadau Park, a beautiful garden on the shore of Lake Thun. Here, we can also see the famous Thun-Panorama. A Swiss artist painted this 360-degree image of the town in 1814.

Finally, we return to the old town and visit one of the many cafés for some coffee and a piece of delicious cake.

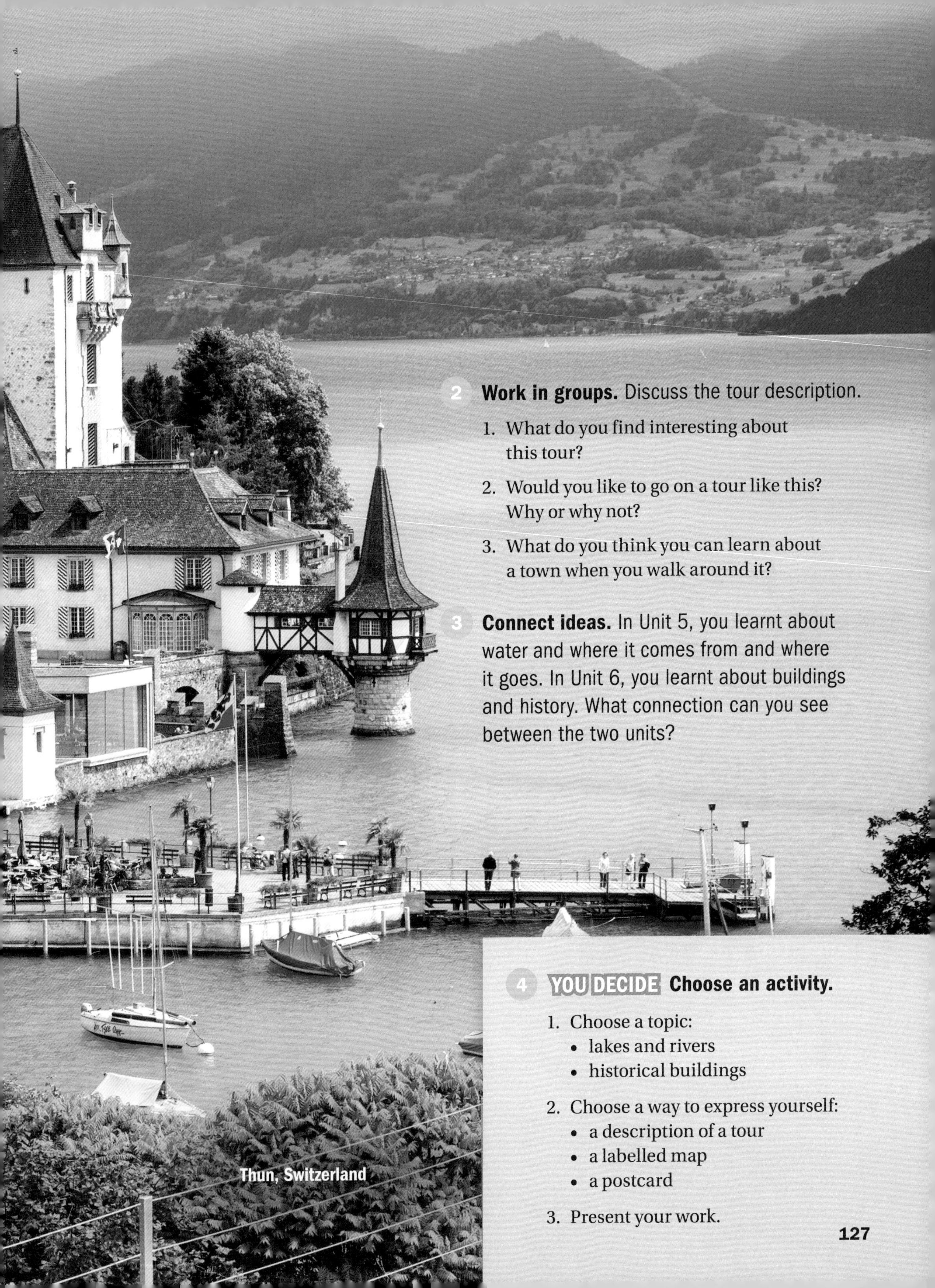

Thun, Switzerland

2 **Work in groups.** Discuss the tour description.

1. What do you find interesting about this tour?
2. Would you like to go on a tour like this? Why or why not?
3. What do you think you can learn about a town when you walk around it?

3 **Connect ideas.** In Unit 5, you learnt about water and where it comes from and where it goes. In Unit 6, you learnt about buildings and history. What connection can you see between the two units?

4 **YOU DECIDE** **Choose an activity.**

1. Choose a topic:
   - lakes and rivers
   - historical buildings
2. Choose a way to express yourself:
   - a description of a tour
   - a labelled map
   - a postcard
3. Present your work.

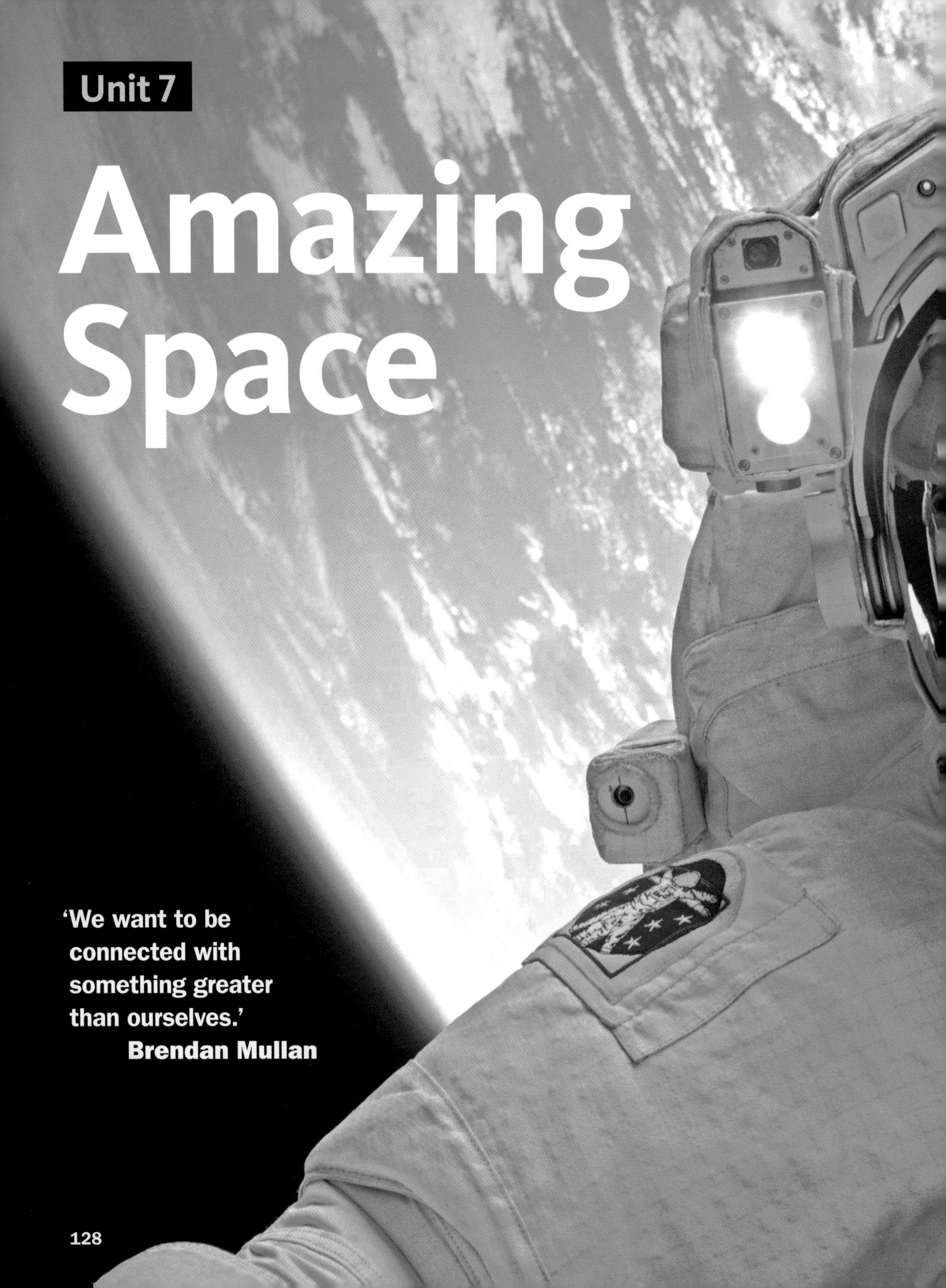

Unit 7

# Amazing Space

'We want to be connected with something greater than ourselves.'
**Brendan Mullan**

NASA astronaut Mike Hopkins on a spacewalk

## TO START

1. Look at the photo. Imagine you are this astronaut. How do you feel at the moment?
2. We see planet Earth in the photo. What other planets can you name? What else is in space?
3. Would you like to travel into space? Why or why not? What do you think are the most difficult things about space travel for astronauts?

**1** **What do you know about space exploration?** Name a space mission or space programme that you know of. Discuss. Then listen and read. 107

We live on the planet Earth. Earth is part of the **solar system**, and it **orbits** the sun. The sun is at the centre of our solar system. Our solar system is a small part of the Milky Way **galaxy**. Our galaxy is one of many millions of galaxies in the **universe**.

In the past, we could only look at the stars and planets through telescopes.

Now, we have the technology to find out about these stars and planets. We can send astronauts into **space**. We also use robot **spacecraft** for very long **journeys** to distant planets in our solar system.

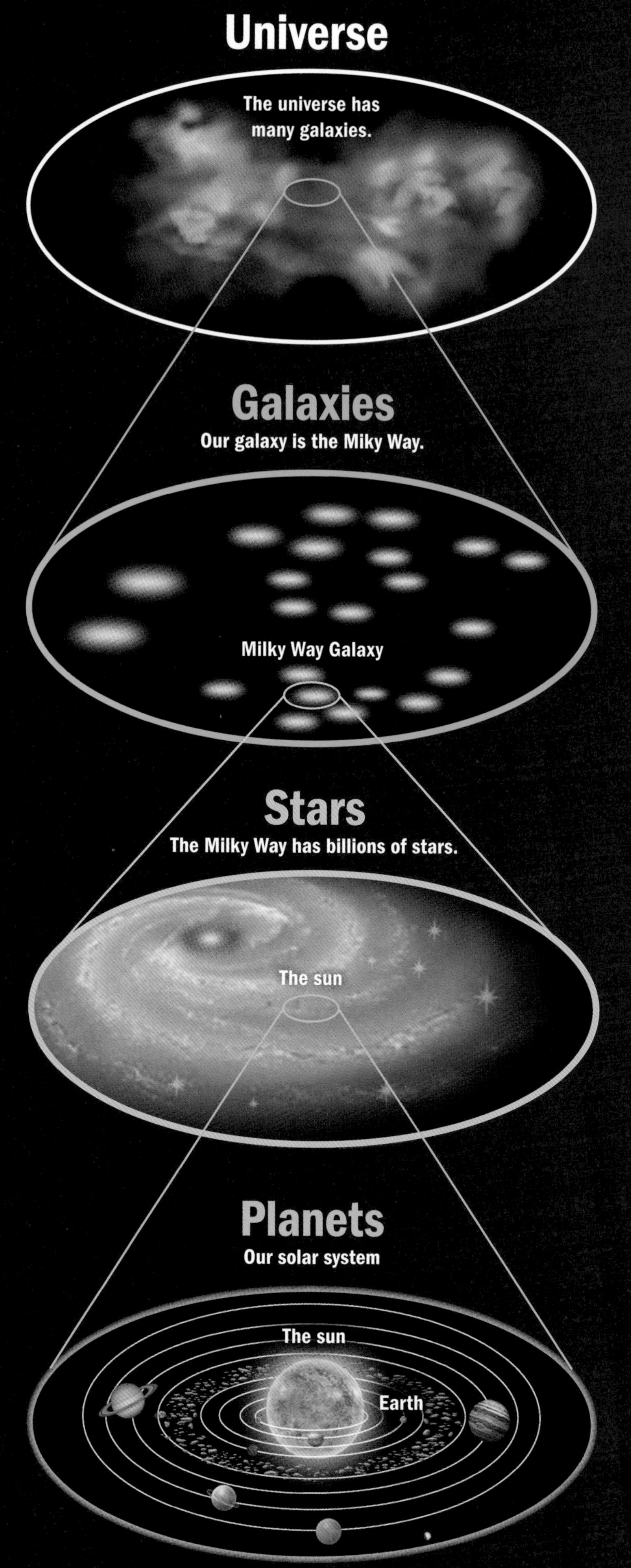

## The Juno Mission

The spacecraft Juno left Earth in August 2011. In July 2016, Juno began to orbit around the **planet** Jupiter. Now, Juno is sending information about Jupiter back to Earth.

Jupiter is the biggest planet in our solar system. Like the sun, its atmosphere is made mainly of two gases – hydrogen and helium.

Juno's mission is a **one-way trip**. It won't return to Earth. In 2018, it will fly into Jupiter and be destroyed.

## The New Horizons Mission

On 19th January 2006, the robot spacecraft New Horizons began its long journey to the very edge of our solar system, just past Neptune. This area is called the Kuiper Belt. It is a ring of icy rocks, some comets and some dwarf planets. One of the dwarf planets is Pluto. New Horizons flew past Pluto in July 2015, and is now **travelling** towards other objects in the Kuiper Belt. The New Horizons mission will help us to understand the outer edge of our solar system.

2 LEARN NEW WORDS **Listen and repeat.** 108

3 **Work in pairs.** Why do you think scientists are so interested in finding out about other planets? How can this knowledge help us on Earth?

**4** **Read and write the words from the list.** Make any necessary changes.

| galaxy | orbit | planet | space | travel | universe |
|---|---|---|---|---|---|

Brendan Mullan fell in love with ________________ when he was ten years old. He went on a school trip to a planetarium. 'I thought it was the coolest thing in the world and decided right there I wanted to know how it all works,' he says. That school trip was the beginning of his career as an astrobiologist. Brendan now teaches physics and astronomy at a university. He also runs astrobiology summer camps for children. He studies how stars form in different ________________. In 2012, Brendan was the American winner of a competition called *FameLab*. For the competition, he had to describe a complex scientific idea in three minutes. Brendan talked about why aliens have never ________________ to Earth. He is very interested in life beyond Earth. He wants to find out if we are alone in the ________________. Is Earth the only ________________ with life on it?

**5** **LEARN NEW WORDS Listen to these words and match them to their definitions.** Then listen and repeat. 109 110

| astronaut | atmosphere | Earth | gas |
|---|---|---|---|

________________ 1. a substance like air

________________ 2. the planet we live on

________________ 3. a person who travels to outer space to work and study

________________ 4. the air that surrounds a planet

Brendan Mullan

**6** **YOU DECIDE Choose an activity.**

1. **Work independently.** There is a planned mission to Mars in 2020. What three items do you put inside the spacecraft? Explain your choices.
2. **Work in pairs.** Imagine you enter a science competition. You must explain a scientific idea in three minutes. Explain your idea to your classmates.
3. **Work in groups.** Brendan Mullan wants to find out if Earth is the only planet with intelligent life on it. What do you think? Discuss and give reasons for your answers.

## SPEAKING STRATEGY 111

### Making and responding to suggestions

| | |
|---|---|
| **I think we should** write a fact sheet about Saturn. | **I'm not so sure**. A fact sheet is quite boring. |
| **Why don't we** make something? | **That could be good**. |
| **What if we make** a model of the solar system? | **Actually, that could work**. |
| **We could also** record some audio with information about it. | **That's a great idea!** |

**1** **Listen.** How do the speakers make and respond to suggestions? Write the phrases you hear. 112

**2** **Read and complete the dialogue.**

Renata: Have you got any ideas for this homework about planets?

Fabio: ____________________ do something about the Kuiper Belt.

Renata: That could ____________________. There's a lot to learn about the Kuiper Belt.

Fabio: ____________________ also include some information about the New Horizons mission.

Renata: ____________________ about that. I think it's quite difficult to find information about it.

Fabio: ____________________ look on NASA's website?

Renata: ____________________. I'm sure we can find out something about it there.

**3** **Work in pairs.** Spin the wheel. Take turns making suggestions. Your partner will respond to your suggestions.

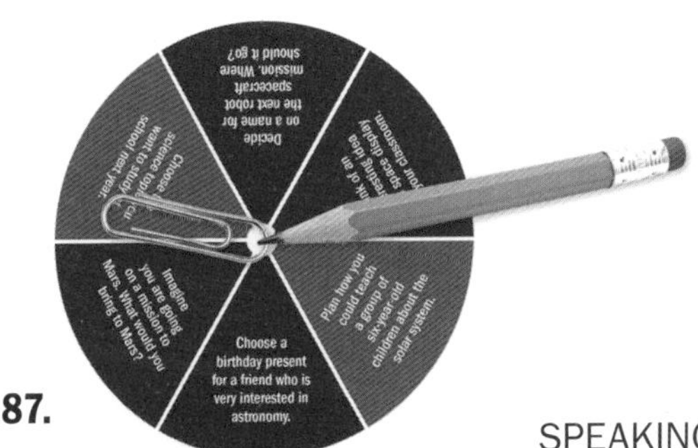


**Go to page 187.**

## GRAMMAR 113

### Comparatives: Comparing two things

Saturn is much **bigger than** Earth, but it's **smaller than** Jupiter.

Saturn is **further** from the sun than Earth. Jupiter is **closer** to the sun than Saturn.

Astronomy is **more interesting than** I thought!

big → bigger

close → closer

interesting → more interesting

small → smaller

far → further

**1 Read.** Complete the sentences with the correct form of the words in the box.

| big | close | cold | far | hot | long | short | small |
|---|---|---|---|---|---|---|---|

**Size:** Venus: 12,104 km (7,521 mi) Earth: 12,756 km (7,926 mi)

1. Venus is ______________________ than Earth.
2. Earth is ______________________ than Venus.

**Length of one day:** Venus: 243 Earth days Earth: 1 Earth day

3. One day on Venus is ______________________ than one day on Earth.
4. One day on Earth is ______________________ than one day on Venus.

**Average temperature:** Venus: 462°C (864°F) Earth: 14.6°C (58.3°F)

5. Venus is much ______________________ than Earth.
6. Earth is much ______________________ than Venus.

**Distance from the sun:** Venus: 108 million km (67 million mi)
Earth: 150 million km (93 million mi)

7. Venus is ______________________ to the sun than Earth.
8. Earth is ______________________ from the sun than Venus.

**2 Work in pairs.** Use the information from the table below to make comparisons between Mercury and Uranus.

Mercury is smaller than Uranus.

| | Size | Distance from the sun | Average temperature | Length of one day |
|---|---|---|---|---|
| **Mercury** | 4,879 km | 58 million km | 167°C (333°F) | 58 Earth days |
| **Uranus** | 51,118 km | 2,871 million km | -197°C (-323°F) | 17 Earth hours |

**3 LEARN NEW WORDS Listen to learn about Jupiter.** Then listen and repeat. 114 115

Jupiter doesn't have a solid **surface**. Its atmosphere is mainly made up of the gases hydrogen and helium.

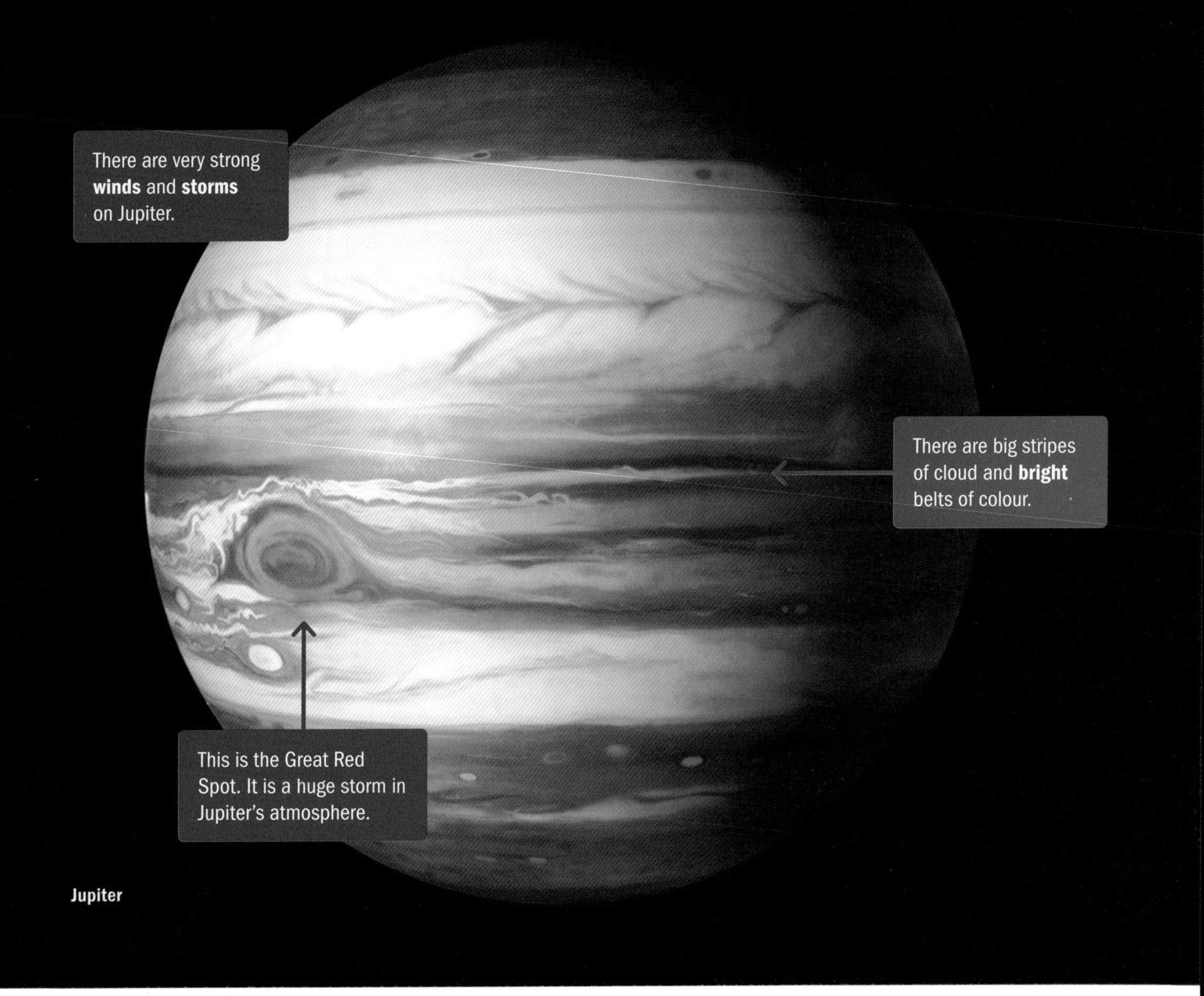


Jupiter

**4 Work in pairs.** Imagine you are an astronomer from another planet, looking at Earth. Compare Earth with your planet using the words in the box.

> I can see that Earth has bright blue oceans. My planet doesn't have oceans on its surface.

| atmosphere | big | bright blue | life | small | solid | storms | surface |
|---|---|---|---|---|---|---|---|

1 BEFORE YOU READ **Discuss in pairs.** What do you know about satellites around Earth? Write a list of uses for satellites.

2 LEARN NEW WORDS **Find these words in the reading.** What do you think they mean? Which of these words are synonyms for *picture* and *find*? Then listen and repeat. 116

| discover | image | lost | signal |
|---|---|---|---|

3 WHILE YOU READ **Look for the different uses of satellites.** 117

4 AFTER YOU READ **Look at these sentences.** Tick T for *True* or F for *False*.

1. GPS is a type of satellite orbiting Earth. T F
2. We use satellite signals to watch TV programmes from anywhere in the world. T F
3. Conservationists in Malaysia use satellite tags to find out information about hawksbill turtles. T F
4. Sarah Parcak uses powerful cameras to take photos of satellites in space. T F
5. Tanis is the name of a new city in Egypt. T F

5 **Work in pairs.** Look at your list from Activity 1. Were any of your ideas included in the article? Can you add any more uses for satellites to the list?

6 **Discuss in groups.**

1. Think about your daily activities. When do you use satellites for information or entertainment?
2. Imagine that all the satellites orbiting Earth suddenly stop working. Think about how this affects people, businesses and transport.
3. Discuss how these people might use information from satellite signals in their daily work: fishermen, pilots, soldiers, world leaders and farmers.

# Satellites Above

## HOW SPACE TECHNOLOGY IS HELPING EARTH

Imagine you are on a long hike with some friends and you get lost. How do you find your way home? If you have a smartphone, you can use it to find your way home. Your phone has a Global Positioning System (GPS). The GPS sends and receives signals from satellites orbiting Earth. It uses information from these satellites to work out exactly where you are and show you how to get home.

Satellites are now part of our daily lives. There are more than 1,000 satellites orbiting Earth at the moment, sending and receiving signals. We use information from these satellites to help us find places, predict the weather and make telephone calls. We can use satellite dishes on our houses to watch satellite TV programmes from anywhere in the world.

In Malaysia, conservationists use satellites to help hawksbill turtles. Hawksbill turtles are critically endangered, and conservationists want to know more about them. The conservationists put satellite tags on the backs of hawksbill turtles. As the turtles swim from place to place in the ocean, the tags send signals to the satellites using GPS. This gives conservationists important information about where turtles go. The conservationists can then work to protect those habitats.

We also use satellites to help us learn more about our planet's history. Archaeologist Sarah Parcak uses powerful space cameras on satellites to take photos of important archaeological sites. She then looks at the images very carefully to find signs of underground buildings and roads. 'From space you can see a detailed network of streets and houses,' she explains. She used this method to discover the underground city of Tanis, in Egypt. 'Now we have a completely new plan of an ancient city no one has seen for 3,000 years.'

Sarah believes that satellite technology can become even more accurate. 'It's getting much better, much faster ... this is the unbelievable future of archaeology.'

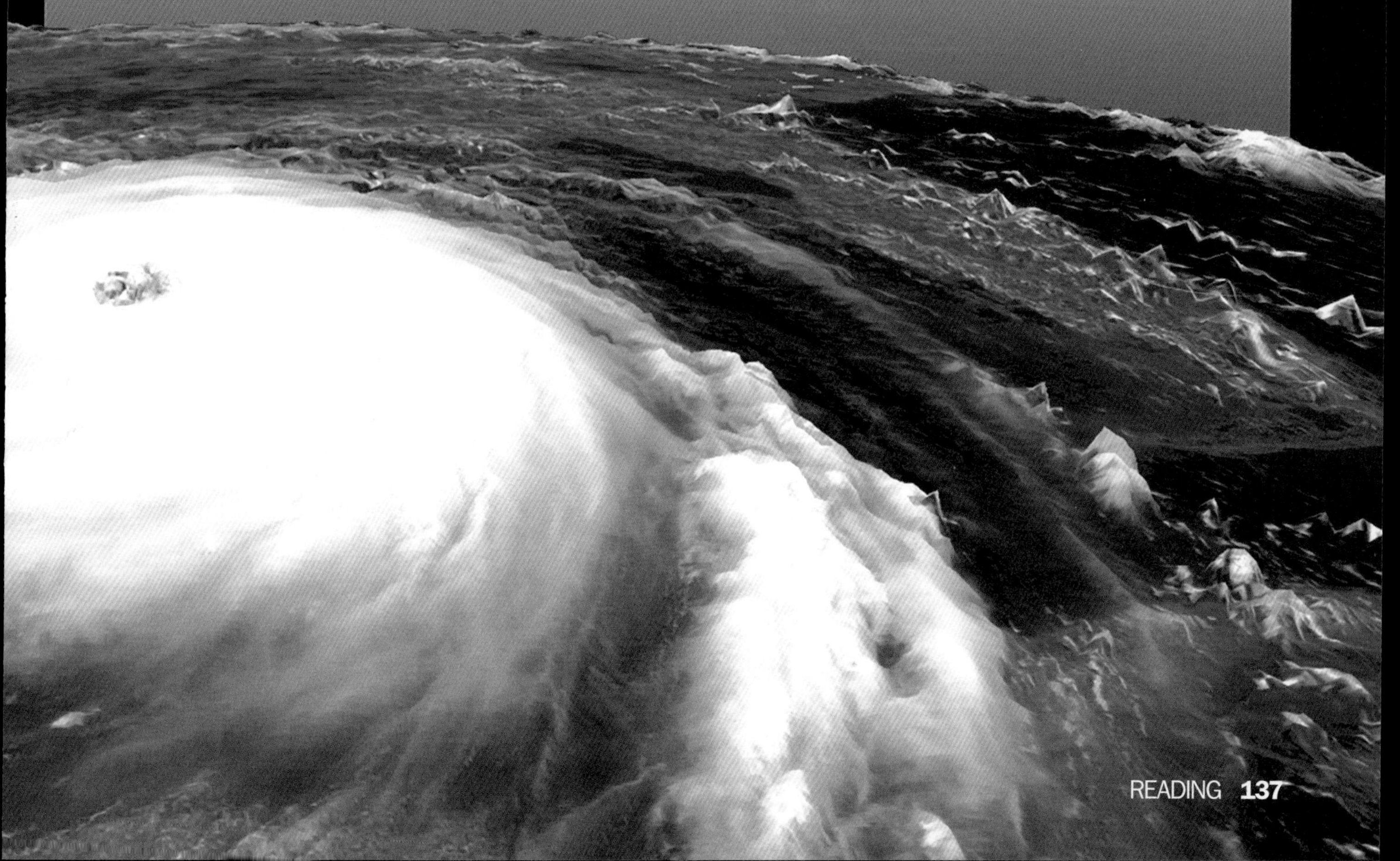

# VIDEO

1 **BEFORE YOU WATCH Discuss in pairs.** Read the definition of *gravity* below. Then think of some other examples that show the force of gravity in everyday life.

*Gravity is a strong force. It pulls things down to the centre of the planet. For example, when you drop a ball, it falls down onto the ground. It doesn't float in the air or rise up. This is because of gravity.*

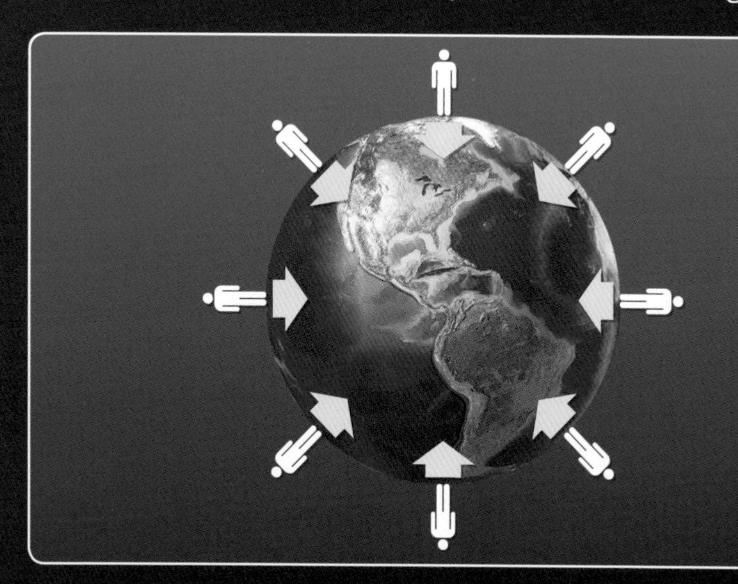

2 **Work in pairs.** You are going to watch *The Electric Wind of Venus*. What do you already know about Venus? Compare it with some of the other planets in the solar system. Look at the diagram on page 133 to remind you.

3 **WHILE YOU WATCH Circle the correct answers.** Watch scene 7.1.

1. Venus is much *wetter* / *drier* than Earth.
2. Venus is much *hotter* / *colder* than Earth.
3. Every planet has *oxygen* / *a gravity field*.
4. Venus has got a very *weak* / *strong* electric field.
5. The electrical field on Venus takes the *oxygen* / *gravity* out of the atmosphere and sends it into space.

The 'electric wind' of Venus

**4** AFTER YOU WATCH **Work in pairs to answer the questions.**

1. Where does Glyn Collinson work?
2. What's the temperature on the surface of Venus?
3. Which two forces does Glyn talk about?
4. Why do you think this discovery about Venus is important?

**5** **Work in groups.** At the end of the video, Glyn talks about looking for habitable planets – planets where life can exist – around other stars. What makes a planet habitable? Make a list of the most important things.

**6** YOU DECIDE **Choose an activity.**

1. **Work independently.** Find out six more facts about Venus. Then compare Venus with Earth.
2. **Work in pairs.** Find out about gravity and the atmosphere on one of the other planets in our solar system. Present your information to the class.
3. **Work in groups.** Find different objects and drop them onto the ground from the same height. Time how long it takes for each object to hit the ground. Discuss your results. What affects how quickly an object falls?

## GRAMMAR 118

**Superlatives: Comparing three or more things**

I learnt many interesting facts about space in my science class. The **most interesting** facts were about stars.

Canopus is brighter than Rigil Kentaurus, but **the brightest** star in our night sky is Sirius.

Proxima Centauri is closer to Earth than Barnard's Star, but **the closest** star to Earth is the sun.

Jupiter is bigger than Saturn, but **the biggest object** in our solar system is the sun.

bright → brighter → the brightest
big → bigger → the biggest
close → closer → the closest
interesting → more interesting → the most interesting

**1** **Read.** Complete the sentences with the correct form of the word in brackets.

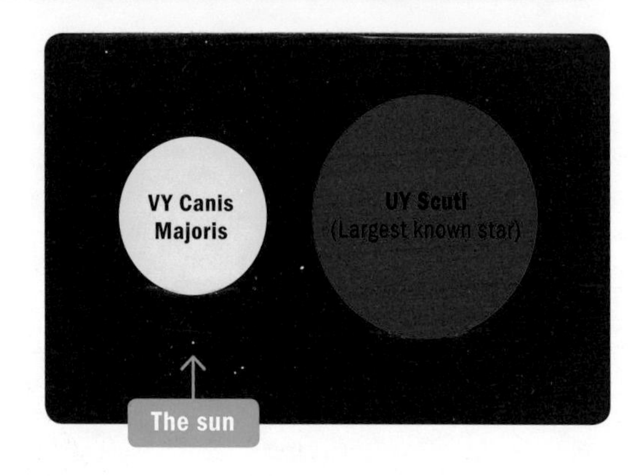


There are billions of stars in our galaxy and billions of galaxies in the universe. It's impossible to know about all of these stars. Here are some facts that scientists like Brendan Mullan know today about the stars we can see in the universe. As we watch new stars form, our knowledge may change in the future.

1. The brown dwarf star called WISE J085510.83-071442.5 is ________________ (cool) star ever found.
2. ________________ (big) star in the universe is UY Scuti. It is 1,700 times bigger than the sun!
3. ________________ (small) known star today is OGLE-TR-122b, a red dwarf star.
4. ________________ (bright) stars in the universe are blue hypergiants, like Eta Carinae. These are also ________________ (hot) stars in the universe.
5. Scientists believe that ________________ (old) star in the universe is HD 140283, also called the Methuselah Star. They believe this star formed more than 13 billion years ago.
6. The ________________ (close) star to Earth other than the sun is Proxima Centauri.

**2** **Work in pairs.** Take turns choosing a blue card. Make a question from the words on the card. Then try to find the matching answer on a red card.

The ______ (hot) planet in our solar system is Venus.

What / is / hot / planet / in our solar system?

**Go to page 189.**

## WRITING

When we compare and contrast two things, we describe the things that are the same and the things that are different.

> ***Both** Saturn and Jupiter are gas giant planets in our solar system.*
>
> ***Although** Uranus is closer to the sun, it is colder than Neptune.*
>
> *Uranus is several times larger than Earth. Saturn, **however**, is much bigger than Uranus.*
>
> *Earth has one moon, **but** Mars has two moons.*

1 **Read the model.** How does the writer compare and contrast Jupiter and Venus? Underline the words for comparison, and circle the words for contrast.

### Jupiter and Venus

Jupiter and Venus are both planets in our solar system. Jupiter is further from the sun and much bigger than Venus. In fact, Jupiter is the largest planet in the solar system. Venus is a terrestrial planet. This means that it has a solid surface. Jupiter, however, is a gas giant planet and does not have a solid surface. Jupiter has 67 moons in orbit around it, but Venus has no moons. Jupiter also has some rings of small pieces of rock around it. Venus doesn't have any rings around it. Although both Venus and Jupiter have layers of cloud around them, Venus has a much hotter surface temperature than Jupiter. Jupiter's clouds are white, brown and orange, but Venus's clouds are all white.

2 **Read the model again.** Make a table of the similarities and the differences between Venus and Jupiter. Look at the table on page 134 for ideas.

3 **Write.** Compare and contrast Saturn and Mars. Describe the things that are the same and the things that are different about the two planets.

Jupiter

# Think Like a Scientist

**'Ask questions, solve problems, think like a scientist, stay curious!'**

**Brendan Mullan**
**National Geographic Explorer, Astrobiologist**

1. **Watch scene 7.2.**
2. Brendan Mullan says you should 'Think like a scientist.' What do you think he means? How do scientists think? How can you think like a scientist? Give an example of a problem that you solved by thinking like a scientist.
3. What do you want to know about space, the planets and the stars? Make a list of questions. Then think like a scientist and decide how you can find the answers to your questions.

# Make an Impact

**YOU DECIDE** Choose a project.

**1 Write and role-play an interview.**

- Use the Internet to find out about daily life on the International Space Station (ISS).
- Write an interview between a journalist on Earth and an astronaut on the ISS.
- Role-play your interview for the class.

**2 Give a presentation about a planet.**

- In a group, choose one of the planets in our solar system.
- Create a presentation with information about the planet. Include pictures, photos and facts.
- Give the presentation to the class and answer their questions about it.

**3 Make a timeline of a famous astronaut's life.**

- Find out about the life of a famous astronaut.
- Create a timeline to show the astronaut's important life events. Find or draw pictures for each event.
- Present your timeline to the class. Explain why you chose this astronaut.

NASA astronaut Mae C Jemison

# See the World

'If you are passionate about what you do, it makes motivating yourself and working hard much easier.'

**Sarah McNair-Landry**

Expedition team members trek over blue glacial ice

## TO START

1. Look at the photo. Do you want to travel to this place? Why or why not?
2. Why do people travel? Think of different reasons. Why don't some people like to travel?
3. When you travel, how can you get to know local people? How do you think local people feel about travellers from other countries?

**1** **What famous places in China can you name?** Discuss. Then listen and read. 119

Sunset over the Great Wall of China

STUDENT CULTURAL TRIP TO

**5th September – 14th September**

**ITINERARY:**

**DAY 1**

We arrive in Beijing and check into our beautiful old Hutong hotel in Beijing's Dongcheng district.

**DAY 2**

We join a tour of the Great Wall of China. Make sure you **pack** some comfortable shoes for this part of our **trip** because we're going to do a lot of hiking today!

**DAY 3**

In the morning, we visit the Forbidden City. In the afternoon, we travel to the 2008 Beijing Olympic sites. In the evening, we enjoy some traditional Chinese opera at the Lao She Tea House.

**DAY 4**

We experience China's amazing **public transport** system when we go **by** high-speed **train** to Shanghai. Later, we check into our hotel in the Pudong area of Shanghai.

**DAY 5**

We travel **by boat** down the Huangpu River in the morning. In the afternoon, we visit the Shanghai Museum.

**DAY 6**

Today is our chance to buy gifts for our families at the Shanghai Historic District – a very popular shopping area for **tourists**.

**DAY 7**

We travel **by coach** to Nanjing. We stay with local families and experience traditional Chinese food and friendship!

**DAY 8**

We **spend** the day at Nanjing No. 1 Junior Middle School and take part in some lessons.

**DAY 9**

We visit Xuanwu Lake and Jiming Temple. In the evening, we have a goodbye dinner with students from Nanjing No. 1 Junior Middle School.

**DAY 10**

The coach to the **airport leaves** at 7 a.m., so we have a very early breakfast. It's time to say goodbye to China and begin our journey home!

**MOST IMPORTANT ITEMS TO PACK:**

* **Tickets**
* **Passport**
* Comfortable shoes
* Warm clothes
* Spending money (no more than £30)

2 LEARN NEW WORDS **Listen and repeat.** 120

3 **Work in pairs.** Imagine that this is the itinerary for your school trip to China next week. How do you feel about the trip? Which activities are you looking forward to? Which parts of the trip are you worried about?

**4** **Read and write the words from the list.** Make any necessary changes.

| airport | by | left | pack | spent | tourists | trip |
|---|---|---|---|---|---|---|

Sarah McNair-Landry loves to travel, but she's not like most ______________________. She goes on long expeditions to places like the North and South Poles, the Gobi Desert, the Sahara and Greenland. In 2015, she and Erik Boomer ______________________ 120 days in the Canadian Arctic. They ______________________ Sarah's home town of Iqualuit in February 2015 and and travelled around Baffin Island ______________________ dogsled. They ______________________ a lot of food for the journey, including 30 kg (66 lb) of chocolate! Baffin Island is the fifth largest island in the world, and Sarah and Erik's journey was 4,000 km (2,500 mi) long. Sarah's parents did the same ______________________ 25 years earlier.

Sarah McNair-Landry

**5** **LEARN NEW WORDS Listen to these words and use them to complete the sentences.** Then listen and repeat. 121 122

| gift | hotel | local | tour |
|---|---|---|---|

1. A ______________________ person or place is part of the area.
2. You often give a ______________________ to someone on their birthday.
3. You can stay in a ______________________ when you're on holiday.
4. When you go on a ______________________ you visit several different places.

**6** **YOU DECIDE** **Choose an activity.**

1. **Work independently.** Imagine that you can interview Sarah McNair-Landry about one of her expeditions. Which expedition do you want to ask about? Make a list of questions.
2. **Work in pairs.** Interview each other about your most interesting travel experience. Explain why it was interesting and what you learnt.
3. **Work in groups.** Which places in your area are interesting for tourists? Think of three different places for students from another country to visit. Discuss why they should visit these places.

## SPEAKING STRATEGY 123

### Asking for and giving directions

| | |
|---|---|
| **Where is** the Town Hall? | It's **on the corner of** Cumberland Street and King Street. |
| **How do I get** there from the Fishermen's Memorial? | **Go straight down** King Street. **Turn left** when you get to Cumberland Street. It's **on the right**. |
| **Do you know how to get to** Fox Street from the Lunenburg Academy? | **Go down** Unity Lane. **Turn right** into Cornwall Street. **Take the first left** into Fox Street. |

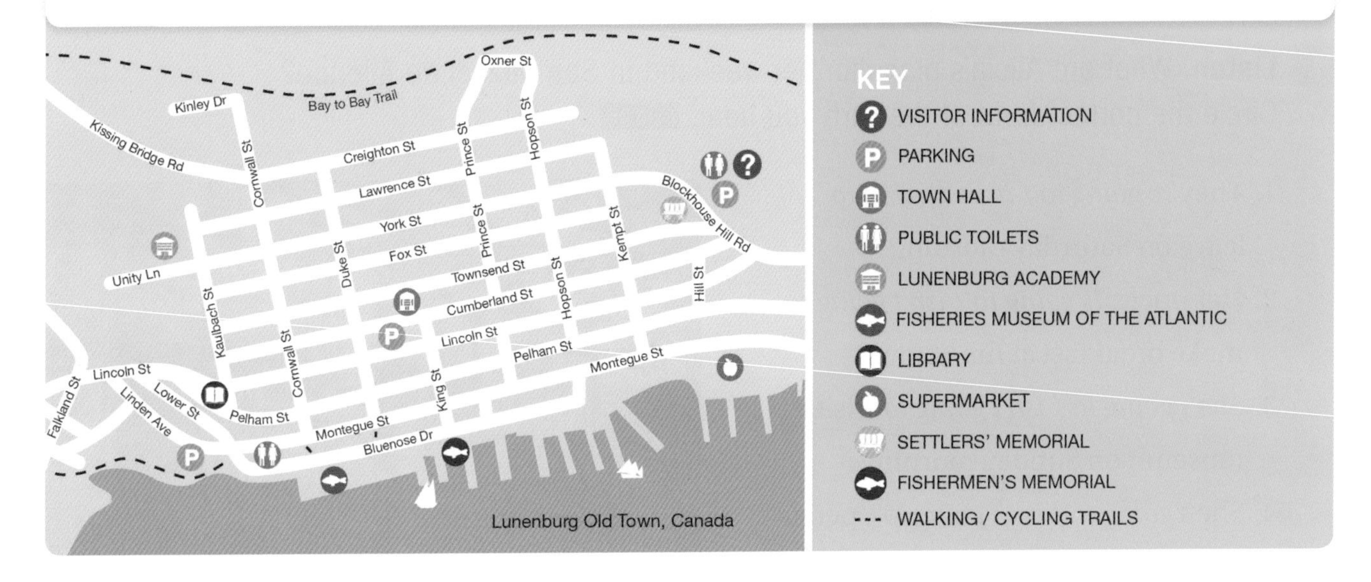


1 **Listen.** The speakers are at the Town Hall. How do they ask for and give directions? Write the phrases you hear. 124

2 **Read and complete the dialogue.** The speakers are at the Town Hall.

Rosa: Excuse me, ______________________ the library?

Marley: The library? That's ______________________ of Pelham Street and Kaulbach Street.

Rosa: ______________________?

Marley: From Cumberland Street, ______________________ King Street. ______________________ into Lincoln Street. Go ______________________ Lincoln Street, and ______________________ when you get to Kaulbach Street. The library is ______________________.

Rosa: Great, thank you!

3 **Work in pairs.** Use the map on this page. Start at the library. Take turns. Pick a card. Ask for directions to the place on the card.

**Go to page 191.**

## GRAMMAR 125

***Going to:* Describing future plans**

**What are you going to do for your birthday**?

I**'m going to spend** the weekend in San Miguel de Allende. My uncle lives there.

We **aren't going to go** by train. My brother**'s going to drive**.

On Saturday, my uncle**'s going to take** us on a tour of the town.

On Sunday, we**'re going to have** a picnic at the Botanical Gardens.

1 **Listen.** What are Alicia's plans for her weekend in San Miguel de Allende? Circle the correct form of the verb you hear. 126

1. They*'re going to / aren't going to* leave on Saturday morning.
2. Her uncle *is going to / isn't going to* make breakfast at his home.
3. She*'s going to / isn't going to* visit a museum on Sunday morning.
4. She*'s going to / isn't going to* spend some time at her uncle's house on Sunday afternoon.
5. They*'re going to / aren't going to* drive home on Sunday evening.

San Miguel de Allende, Mexico

2 **Work in groups.** Complete the text about Ricardo's plans for Sunday.

Ricardo ______________ (not visit) the museum with Alicia on Sunday morning. He ______________ (go) by bus to Fábrica La Aurora – a place with a lot of art galleries. He ______________ (look for) a surprise birthday gift for his sister there. Then, he ______________ (walk) to San Agustín Café. He ______________ (buy) a special cake for his sister there. Then he and his uncle ______________ (give) the gift and the cake to his sister at the Botanical Gardens.

3 **Work in pairs.** Imagine that a friend from another town is going to visit you this weekend. What are you going to do together? Discuss your plans.

In the morning, we're going to go to the sports centre.

**4** **LEARN NEW WORDS Listen to learn about two UNESCO World Heritage sites: Hạ Long Bay and Göreme National Park.** Then listen and repeat. 127 128

Islands of Hạ Long Bay, Vietnam

Hạ Long Bay in Vietnam is famous for its many small **islands**. Tourists enjoy travelling by boat from one island to another, admiring the beautiful **beaches** and green forests.

In Göreme National Park in Turkey, there are mountains, **valleys**, **caves** and underground cities in the rock. Tourists can stay in hotels in the caves.

Göreme National Park, Central Anatolia, Turkey

**5** **Work in groups.** Imagine you can choose one of these three places for your next holiday: San Miguel De Allende, Göreme National Park or Hạ Long Bay. Which place are you going to visit and why? What are you going to do there?

1 BEFORE YOU READ **Discuss in pairs.** Look at the title and the photo. What do you think the reading is about?

2 **LEARN NEW WORDS Look at the words below.** What do you think they mean? Now find them in the reading. Has your idea about the meaning changed? Explain. Then listen and repeat. 129

**equipment** **pull** **snow shovel** **tent**

3 WHILE YOU READ **Try to picture the events of Sarah and Eric's journey in your mind.** 130

4 AFTER YOU READ **Work in pairs to answer the questions.**

1. Why did people in the past want to use the Northwest Passage?
2. Which days were easier for Sarah and Eric – windy days or days with no wind?
3. Why did Sarah and Eric change their route at Boothia Strait?
4. How did Sarah make the polar bear go away?
5. How did the people of Pond Inlet welcome Sarah and Eric?

5 **Work in pairs.** Choose one paragraph from the text. Draw a picture to show what happened to Eric and Sarah.

6 **Discuss in groups.**

1. For this journey, Sarah and Eric travelled by kite-ski. Think about the advantages and disadvantages of travelling by kite-ski. Would you like to travel this way? Why or why not?
2. For many days of their trip, Sarah and Eric were alone in the middle of the Arctic. What are the dangers of travelling so far from a town or village? Why do you think people like travelling in remote locations?
3. Imagine you are planning a journey with an unusual means of transport. Explain why you want to travel this way and where you want to go.

**Sarah McNair-Landry kite-skiing across the Northwest Passage of Canada**

# Kite-skiing in the Arctic

## Polar bears, melting ice and a lot of chocolate!

**The Northwest Passage is a sea route along the Arctic coast of Canada and Alaska. It connects the Atlantic and the Pacific Oceans. In the past, many explorers tried to sail through the Northwest Passage because it was a much shorter route from China to Europe. The freezing ice made travelling by sea very dangerous and difficult.**

In 2011, Sarah McNair-Landry and her brother, Eric, decided to kite-ski 3,300 km (2,500 mi) across the frozen Northwest Passage in Canada. They each took four kites – big kites for days when there wasn't much wind, and small kites for days when the wind was very strong. Of course, they also packed sleeping bags, a tent and a lot of food, including 200 bars of chocolate! In total, they had four sledges, with about 180 kg (400 lb) of equipment. Sarah and Eric were on skis for the journey.

On windy days, the kites pulled Sarah and Eric (on their skis) and the sledges with all the equipment. But on days when there was no wind, they had to pull the sledges themselves with no help. Sometimes, when the weather was really bad, they only travelled 5–6 km (3–4 mi) per day.

Sarah and Eric started their journey in the west, in Tuktoyaktuk. Along the route, they stopped at seven small communities, where they stayed with local families. They visited the schools at each community and talked to the children about their trip.

One of the most difficult parts of their trip was at Boothia Strait. The ice started to melt, and Sarah and Eric had to change their route. They decided to camp for the night and make a new plan the next day.

At four o'clock in the morning, Sarah woke up suddenly. There was a polar bear outside the tent and it wanted to come inside! Eric tried to scare it away with a snow shovel, but the snow shovel was very small and the polar bear was very big! Then Sarah found her rifle and shot it once above the bear's head. The bear ran away, but Sarah and Eric didn't go back to sleep. They wanted to leave. On the same morning, they saw five more polar bears.

On 11th June 2011, after 85 days, Sarah and Eric finally arrived at the tiny Inuit community of Pond Inlet. They were very tired, hungry and wet from the melting ice. The Mayor of Pond Inlet greeted them on the beach. In the evening, the local people organised a dance party. It was an amazing end to a wonderful expedition.

**Sarah McNair-Landry's route**

# VIDEO

1 **BEFORE YOU WATCH Discuss in pairs.** Imagine you can take a trip to any country in the world. Which country do you want to go to? Why? What do you want to do there?

2 **Read and tick.** You are going to watch *Student Expedition: Tanzania*. Before you watch, predict which images you will see:

| | | |
|---|---|---|
| ______ cameras | ______ tents | ______ dancing |
| ______ shops | ______ computers | ______ singing |
| ______ elephants | ______ caves | ______ boats |
| ______ stars | | |

National Geographic Student Expedition, Tanzania

3 WHILE YOU WATCH **Check your predictions from Activity 2. Watch scene 8.1.**

4 AFTER YOU WATCH **Work in pairs.** Tick T for *True* or F for *False*.

1. The boy thought a trip to Tanzania would change his life. T F
2. The boy believes that he can use his camera to take photos of all the new things he sees in Tanzania. T F
3. The boy thinks that the trip was a typical tourist experience. T F
4. The girl came to Tanzania to learn about a different culture and lifestyle and to improve her photography skills. T F
5. The girl's favourite animal is a lion. T F

5 **Work in groups.** Would you like to take part in an expedition like this? Why or why not? Which parts of the video looked most interesting or exciting? Think of some problems or difficulties you might have on this kind of expedition.

6 **Work in pairs.** In the video, one of the students says, 'I can honestly say that a part of me is changed because I came to Tanzania.' How do you think a trip to another country might change your life?

7 YOU DECIDE **Choose an activity.**

1. **Work independently.** Imagine you are in Tanzania on a National Geographic Student Expedition. Write a postcard home to your family about your activities in the last few days.
2. **Work in pairs.** Find out about a National Geographic Student Expedition to another country. Write a short description of it.
3. **Work in groups.** Prepare a short holiday brochure about Tanzania. Find out about four popular activities for tourists. Find photos to go with your information. Present your brochure to the class.

## GRAMMAR 131

***In, on* and *at*: Saying when things happen**

**On Friday,** we're going to fly to Prague.

**On Saturday morning,** we're going to see Prague Castle.

**At lunchtime,** we're going to try the new café in Wenceslas Square.

**In the afternoon,** I'm going to walk to the Alfons Mucha Museum.

**At seven o'clock in the evening,** we're going to meet our friends at Prague Estates Theatre.

**1 Read.** Complete the email with *in*, *on* or *at*.

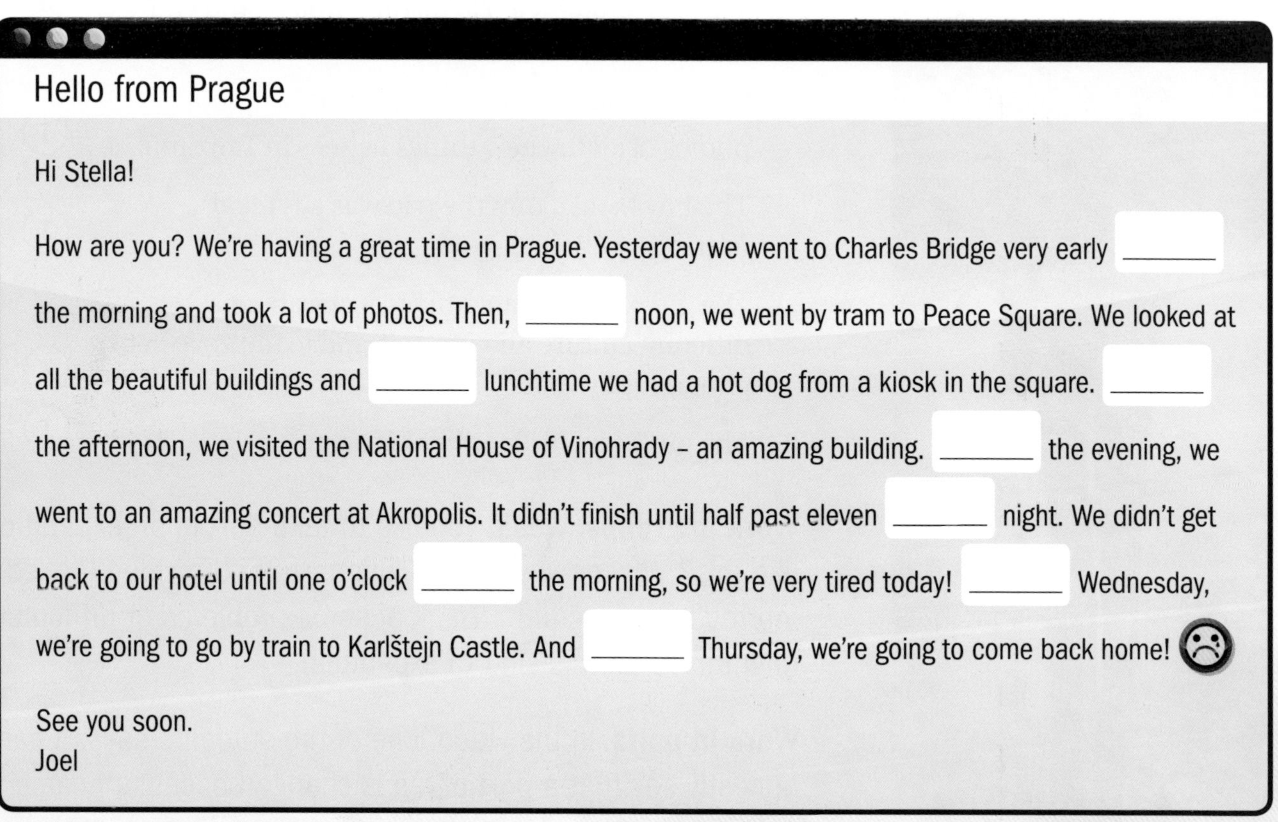

Hello from Prague

Hi Stella!

How are you? We're having a great time in Prague. Yesterday we went to Charles Bridge very early ______ the morning and took a lot of photos. Then, ______ noon, we went by tram to Peace Square. We looked at all the beautiful buildings and ______ lunchtime we had a hot dog from a kiosk in the square. ______ the afternoon, we visited the National House of Vinohrady – an amazing building. ______ the evening, we went to an amazing concert at Akropolis. It didn't finish until half past eleven ______ night. We didn't get back to our hotel until one o'clock ______ the morning, so we're very tired today! ______ Wednesday, we're going to go by train to Karlštejn Castle. And ______ Thursday, we're going to come back home! ☹

See you soon.
Joel

**2 Work in pairs.** Talk about your plans for the next two or three days. Use *in*, *on* and *at*.

**3 Work in pairs.** Spin the wheel. Take turns making sentences using the words on the wheel and the correct preposition: *in*, *on* or *at*.

I had a cheese sandwich at lunchtime.

**Go to page 187.**

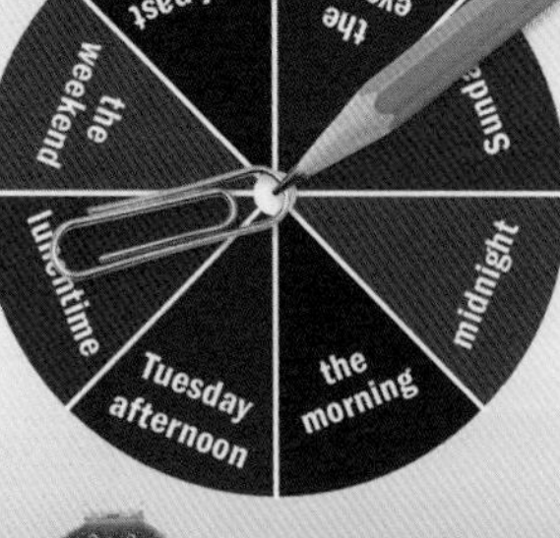


Prague, Czech Republic

## WRITING

Blogs usually include the following information:

- **The titles of the blog posts**
- **The date of each blog post**
- **A small piece of information about the author (the *blogger*)**

At the end of the blog post, the blogger often asks the readers to add their comments.

1 **Read the model.** Work in pairs to identify and underline these four things: the title of the blog post, the date of the blog post, the information about the blogger and the request for comments.

# My Life, My Music, My World, My Blog!

12th December 2016

About me: I'm Mateo. I'm from Córdoba and I love music, football and empanadas!

**My Staycation**

Every summer holiday our family goes away for a week or two. Sometimes we visit friends in the mountains or we go to the beach. Sometimes we travel to other countries. This year, we're going to do something completely different. We're going to have a 'staycation'. We're planning to stay at home and explore all the exciting things right here in Córdoba, Argentina.

On Monday, we're going to visit the Paseo del Buen Pastor. We're planning to look at some modern art and listen to some music. On Tuesday, we're going to have a picnic at Parque Sarmiento and in the evening my sister's hoping to take a tango lesson. (I'm not so sure about that plan!) On Wednesday, we're planning to make a day trip to a small town near Córdoba called Cosquín. We're going to listen to some folk music there. After that ... I don't know yet. But there's so much to do in my own city, I think a staycation is a great idea!

What do you think of our staycation plans? Please comment below!

**Fountain show, Paseo de Buen Pastor, Córdoba, Argentina**

2 **Work in pairs.** Do you like the idea of a staycation? Why or why not?

3 **Write.** Write a blog about your holiday plans. Include all of the information you usually find on a blog.

# Get Outside!

**'Get outside and have fun!'**

**Sarah McNair-Landry**
**National Geographic Explorer, Adventurer and Cinematographer**

1. **Watch scene 8.2.**
2. What things can you learn about when you travel to a different place? What can you learn about yourself?
3. Think about a time that you spent outside recently. What did you do? What did you see? What did you learn? Did you have fun?

# Make an Impact

**YOU DECIDE** **Choose a project.**

**1 Create a tour itinerary.**

- Make a list of interesting places in your local area.
- Design a three-day tour itinerary for visitors. Think about how they can get from one place to the next. Use photos to illustrate your itinerary.
- Present your itinerary to the class and answer their questions about it.

**2 Write a blog entry.**

- Research a city in another country.
- Pretend that you are on holiday in this city. Write a blog about your visit. Include photos.
- Publish your blog. Answer questions and respond to your classmates' comments.

**3 Make a map.**

- Survey your friends and family to find out which places around the world they have visited.
- Draw or print out a map of the world and label each place with the name of the person who went there and information about why they went there.
- Show your map to the class. Discuss which places are the most popular and why.

# Express Yourself

**1** **Read and listen to the blog.** 132

## Welcome to Haneul's Awesome Blogging World

**23rd May 2028** I saw the competition in a science magazine: 'Win a five-day holiday in a space hotel, 300 km (186 mi) above Earth.' A holiday like that costs more than $1 million. Of course I entered the competition! I'm crazy about space. And ... can you believe it? I won! Now, I am in a rocket with five billionaires on our way into space!

**24th May 2028** The journey on the rocket yesterday was quite scary and very noisy. It was also much faster than I imagined. In fact, it only took ten minutes to get into space, but it took six hours to connect with our space hotel. The space hotel is amazing! We all have our own bedrooms, and we have special straps to hold us onto our beds so we don't float away when we're asleep! It's really strange being in zero gravity.

**25th May 2028** I took a lot of photos today. I think Earth is the most beautiful and the most colourful thing in space. We're travelling around Earth at 27,000 km (16,777 mi) per hour, and we can watch the sun rise and set 16 times a day!

**26th May 2028** Some of the other guests in this space hotel complain about everything! They don't like the food or the beds. But I think we are the luckiest people in the universe!

**27th May 2028** Today was our last day in the space hotel. Now I just need to find $1 million for my next trip!

How do you think the guests spend their time there?

2. Haneul describes his experiences in a blog. What else can you read to find out about travel? How do you learn about other places?

3 **Connect ideas.** In Unit 7, you learnt about space. In Unit 8, you learnt about travel. What connection do you see between the two units?

Plans for a future space hotel

4 **YOU DECIDE Choose an activity.**

1. Choose a topic:
   - space travel
   - an unusual holiday
2. Choose a way to express yourself:
   - a blog
   - a short story
   - a poem
3. Present your work.

# Unit 1

## Syllables and stress

1 **Listen.** Words in English have one or more parts. Each part is called a *syllable*. Each syllable has a vowel sound in it. It can also have one or more consonant sounds. Listen to the syllables in these words for nationalities. 133

| 1 | 2 | 3 |
|---|---|---|
| **French** | **Ger** - man | Kor - **e** - an |
| | **Spa** - nish | Ja - pan - **ese** |

In words with two or more syllables, one syllable is always stronger than the other. It is pronounced loudly and more clearly. This is called the stressed syllable. Listen again and notice the stressed syllable in the two- and three-syllable words above.

2 **Listen and repeat.** Listen to these words for nationalities. How many syllables do they have? Write *2* or *3* for the number of syllables. 134

1. Taiwanese ___3___
2. English ______
3. Chilean ______
4. Indian ______
5. Chinese ______
6. Russian ______

3 **Work in pairs.** Listen again and repeat the words. Underline the stressed syllable in each word. 135

# Unit 2

## The third person *-s* and *-es* endings

1 **Listen.** Notice the different pronunciation of the -s ending of these three verbs. 136

writes plays teaches

The *-s* verb ending has three possible pronunciations:

- a soft *s* after words ending in *-p, -t, -k* and *-f*
- a hard *z* after words ending in *-b, -d, -g, -l, -r, -w, -m, -n, -v* and *-y*
- an *iz* sound after words ending in *-s, -ch, -sh, -ge, -ss, -x* and *-z*

We use exactly the same rules for the pronunciation of regular plural nouns.

2 **Listen and repeat.** Then write the words in the correct column. 137

| | | | |
|---|---|---|---|
| crashes | gives | jumps | learns |
| misses | ~~plays~~ | runs | sits |
| speaks | ~~teaches~~ | watches | ~~writes~~ |

| soft *s* | hard *z* | *iz* sound |
|---|---|---|
| writes | plays | teaches |

3 **Work in pairs.** Listen and repeat the sentences. Make sure you pronounce the verb endings correctly. 138

1. Josh studies chess every day.
2. Josh wins a chess championship.
3. Then he loses an important game of chess.
4. He decides to learn a new sport.
5. He thinks it is good to fail sometimes.

# Unit 3

## The *th* sound

**1** **Listen.** Notice the two different ways we pronounce the letters *th.* 139

these, those

three, thousand

- The *th* sound in *these* and *those* is voiced. It is a harder sound.
- The *th* sound in *three* and *thousand* is unvoiced. It is a softer sound.

**2** **Listen and repeat.** Decide if you hear an unvoiced *th* like *three* or a voiced *th* like *these.* Write *U* for unvoiced or *V* for voiced. 140

1. brother ______
2. the ______
3. birthday ______
4. that ______
5. nothing ______
6. month ______
7. father ______
8. thing ______

**3** **Work in pairs.** Listen and repeat the sentences. Make sure you pronounce the *th* sounds correctly. 141

1. I think that boy is your brother.
2. My father's birthday is next month.
3. This is a therapy robot.
4. The maths club at my school is on Thursday.
5. There is something in the bath!

---

# Unit 4

## Short vowel sounds

**1** **Listen.** Notice the pronunciation of the underlined vowels. 142

| a | e | i | o | u |
|---|---|---|---|---|
| camera | red | him | hot | lunch |

In English, we have short vowel sounds and long vowel sounds.

The vowel sound is usually short when there is a single vowel with a consonant before and one or two consonants after the vowel.

**2** **Listen and repeat.** Circle the word that *doesn't* have a short vowel sound. 143

1. camel, man, plane, cat, panda
2. lesson, desk, chess, sell, teach
3. kid, pink, wild, it, insect
4. dolphin, food, stop, dog, forest
5. husband, funny, much, buy, cup

**3** **Work in pairs.** Look at pages 84–85. Find at least one word for each short vowel sound and write it in the correct column.

| a | e | i | o | u |
|---|---|---|---|---|
| | | | | |

# Unit 5

## Long vowel sounds

1 **Listen.** Notice the pronunciation of the underlined vowels. 144

| a | e | i | o | u |
|---|---|---|---|---|
| lake | clean | ice | go | juice |

The vowel sound is usually long:

- when there is a consonant after a single vowel and then the letter *e* after the consonant, e.g. *lake*.
- when there is a vowel at the end of a syllable, e.g. *go*.
- when there are two vowels together. We usually pronounce the first vowel as a long vowel sound and the second vowel sound is silent, e.g. *juice*.

2 **Listen and repeat.** Circle the words with long vowel sounds. Underline the words with short vowel sounds. 145

1. fail, same, ape, rain, tap, bag, safe
2. read, easy, bed, week, sea, we, fresh
3. fish, kite, die, sky, drink, wife, twice
4. cloth, snow, code, road, phone, stop, no
5. rude, blue, up, use, school, fun, cool

3 **Work in pairs.** Listen and repeat the sentences. Make sure you pronounce the long and short vowels correctly. 146

1. There's no snow on the road today, so we're going to school.
2. There are five fish in the blue lake.
3. I can see three green kites in the sky.
4. He speaks Greek and French.
5. Don't drink the rain water; it isn't safe!

# Unit 6

## The *n* and *ng* sounds

1 **Listen.** Notice the pronunciation of the endings of these words. 147

| *n* | *ng* |
|---|---|
| thin | thing |
| win | wing |

When we make the *ng* sound, the shape of the tongue in our mouth changes. Listen again and try to copy the sound.

2 **Listen and repeat.** Circle the word you hear. 148

| | |
|---|---|
| 1. ban | bang |
| 2. fan | fang |
| 3. kin | king |
| 4. sin | sing |
| 5. pin | ping |
| 6. ton | tongue |

3 **Work in pairs.** Listen and repeat the sentences. Make sure you pronounce the *ng* sounds correctly. 149

1. The TEA is an amazing building.
2. We're looking at an interesting picture of a modern town.
3. She was a hard-working American woman.
4. I want to learn more about design and engineering.
5. This is a boring museum and the tourists are annoying!

# Unit 7

## The soft and hard *g* sounds

**1** **Listen.** Notice the two different ways we pronounce the letter *g*. 150

gas, galaxy

giant, giraffe

- The *g* sound in *gas* and *galaxy* is a hard *g* sound. There is usually a hard *g* before the vowels -*a*, -*o* and -*u* and before the consonants -*r* and -*l*.
- The *g* sound in *giant* and *giraffe* is a soft *g* sound. There is usually a soft *g* before the vowels -*e* and -*i* or -*y*.

**2** **Listen and repeat.** Decide if you hear a hard *g* or a soft *g*. Write *H* for hard or *S* for soft. 151

1. ground __H__
2. grandfather ____
3. image ____
4. generation ____
5. good ____
6. orange ____
7. grow ____
8. garden ____

**3** **Work in pairs.** Listen and repeat the sentences. Make sure you pronounce the *g* sounds correctly. 152

1. Jupiter is a gas giant planet.
2. I grow oranges and green grapes in my garden.
3. Satellite tags on endangered turtles send signals to satellites using GPS.
4. This is a very good image of an underground city.
5. My granddaughter is studying geography and engineering.

---

# Unit 8

## Silent letters

**1** **Listen.** Many words in English have silent letters. Silent letters are in the written word but are not pronounced in the spoken word. Listen to these words. The underlined letters are the silent letters. 153

write island

listen school

**2** **Listen and repeat.** Listen to these words. Underline the silent letter in each word. 154

1. know
2. wrong
3. hour
4. watch
5. Wednesday
6. design

**3** **Work in pairs.** Listen and repeat the sentences. Make sure you leave out the silent letters. 155

1. We're going to visit the castle tomorrow.
2. Let's eat our sandwiches in the park.
3. On Thursday, I'm going to climb to the top of the mountain.
4. You should come to Minsk in the autumn – it's beautiful then.
5. I want to see the MAXXI museum; Zaha Hadid is my favourite architect.

# Irregular Verbs

| Infinitive | Past simple | Past participle |
|---|---|---|
| be | were | been |
| beat | beat | beaten |
| become | became | become |
| begin | began | begun |
| bend | bent | bent |
| bite | bit | bitten |
| bleed | bled | bled |
| blow | blew | blown |
| break | broke | broken |
| bring | brought | brought |
| build | built | built |
| burn | burnt | burnt |
| buy | bought | bought |
| carry | carried | carried |
| catch | caught | caught |
| choose | chose | chosen |
| come | came | come |
| cost | cost | cost |
| cut | cut | cut |
| deal | dealt | dealt |
| dig | dug | dug |
| do | did | done |
| draw | drew | drawn |
| drink | drank | drunk |
| drive | drove | driven |
| dry | dried | dried |
| eat | ate | eaten |
| fall | fell | fallen |
| feed | fed | fed |
| feel | felt | felt |
| fight | fought | fought |
| find | found | found |
| fly | flew | flown |
| forget | forgot | forgotten |
| forgive | forgave | forgiven |
| freeze | froze | frozen |
| fry | fried | fried |
| get | got | got |
| give | gave | given |
| go | went | gone |
| grow | grew | grown |
| hang | hung | hung |
| have | had | had |
| hear | heard | heard |
| hide | hid | hidden |
| hit | hit | hit |
| hold | held | held |
| hurt | hurt | hurt |
| keep | kept | kept |
| knit | knitted | knitted |
| know | knew | known |

| Infinitive | Past simple | Past participle |
|---|---|---|
| lead | led | led |
| leave | left | left |
| lend | lent | lent |
| let | let | let |
| light | lit | lit |
| lose | lost | lost |
| make | made | made |
| mean | meant | meant |
| meet | met | met |
| pay | paid | paid |
| put | put | put |
| quit | quit | quit |
| read | read | read |
| rise | rose | risen |
| run | ran | run |
| say | said | said |
| see | saw | seen |
| sell | sold | sold |
| send | sent | sent |
| set | set | set |
| sew | sewed | sewn |
| shake | shook | shaken |
| shine | shone | shone |
| show | showed | shown |
| shut | shut | shut |
| sing | sang | sung |
| sink | sank | sunk |
| sit | sat | sat |
| sleep | slept | slept |
| slide | slid | slid |
| speak | spoke | spoken |
| spend | spent | spent |
| spin | spun | spun |
| stand | stood | stood |
| steal | stole | stolen |
| stick | stuck | stuck |
| sting | stung | stung |
| sweep | swept | swept |
| swim | swam | swum |
| swing | swung | swung |
| take | took | taken |
| teach | taught | taught |
| tear | tore | torn |
| tell | told | told |
| think | thought | thought |
| throw | threw | thrown |
| understand | understood | understood |
| wake | woke | woken |
| wear | wore | worn |
| win | won | won |
| write | wrote | written |

# Greetings: Formal and informal

**1 Listen and read.** 156

**Formal**

Linh: Hello, Mrs Tran. How are you?
Mrs Tran: Very well, thank you. And you, Linh?

| Greeting | Responding |
| --- | --- |
| • Hello (Mrs Tran). How are you?<br>• Good morning / afternoon / evening. How are you? | • Very well, thank you. And you?<br>• Fine, thank you. How are you? |

**2 Listen and read.** 157

**Informal**

Linh: Hi, Thao. How are you doing?
Thao: I'm OK, thanks. How are you?

| Greeting | Responding |
| --- | --- |
| • Hi! How are you?<br>• Hello. How's it going?<br>• Hi. How are you doing? | • I'm OK, thanks.<br>• Hi. I'm fine, thanks. How are you?<br>• Great, thanks. How about you?<br>• Not bad, thanks. You? |

# Introductions: Formal and informal

**3** **Listen and read.** 158

**Formal**

Linh: Mrs Tran, I'd like to introduce you to Mai.
Mrs Tran: Hello, Mai. It's a pleasure to meet you.

| Making an introduction | Responding |
|---|---|
| • I'd like to introduce you to Mai.<br>• I'd like you to meet Mai. | • It's a pleasure to meet you, Mai.<br>• I'm very pleased to meet you. |

**4** **Listen and read.** 159

**Informal**

Thao: Hi. My name's Thao. Nice to meet you.
Linh: Hi, Thao. I'm Linh. Very nice to meet you, too.

| Making an introduction | Responding |
|---|---|
| • Hi. I'm Thao.<br>• Hi there. My name's Thao. Nice to meet you.<br>• Hi, Thao. This is Linh. She's in my class.<br>• This is Linh. She's a student at my school. | • Hi, Thao. My name's Linh. Nice to meet you.<br>• Hello. I'm Linh. Very nice to meet you, too.<br>• Hi, Linh. Nice to meet you.<br>• Hi, Linh. I'm Thao. It's nice to meet you. |

# Expressing thanks: Formal and informal

**5 Listen and read.** 160

**Formal**

Mr Silva: You've been very helpful. That's very kind of you.
Lara: It's my pleasure.

| Expressing thanks | Responding |
|---|---|
| • Thank you. That's very kind of you.<br>• Thank you. That's very thoughtful.<br>• I'm very grateful. | • It's my pleasure.<br>• Don't mention it.<br>• It's no trouble at all. |

**6 Listen and read.** 161

**Informal**

Lara: Wow! That's so nice of you. Thanks a lot.
Victor: You're welcome.

| Expressing thanks | Responding |
|---|---|
| • Thanks.<br>• Thanks a lot.<br>• Thanks very much. | • You're welcome.<br>• No problem.<br>• Any time. |

# Taking turns

**7 Listen and read.** 162

Ana: We have to practise the dialogue on page 27. Who should go first?
Lara: Why don't you?
Ana: OK, sure.

| Asking | Responding | Agreeing |
|---|---|---|
| • Who should go first?<br>• Do you want to say the first line?<br>• Who would like to start? | • Why don't you?<br>• I went first the last time.<br>• I'd like to.<br>• Is it OK if I go first? | • OK, sure.<br>• All right.<br>• Of course. |

# Asking for and giving information

## 8 Listen and read. 163

Victor: Hi, Ana. Can you tell me what the maths homework is?
Ana: I think we just need to study for the test.
Victor: I wonder what the test is on ... Do you have any idea?
Ana: I'm not sure, but I think it's on all of Unit 3.

| Asking for information | Responding |
|---|---|
| • Can you tell me ...? | • I think ... |
| • I'd like to know ... | • As far as I know, ... |
| • I wonder ... | • I'm not sure, but I think ... |
| • Do you have any idea? | • I don't know, sorry. |

# Giving a presentation

## 9 Listen and read. 164

Lara: Today, we're going to learn about endangered animals.
Victor: We'll start by describing different endangered animals.
Lara: Have a look at this poster. You'll see that there are a lot of endangered animals in the world.
Victor: Next, let's look at where they come from.
Lara: As you can see, there's a lot to learn! Any questions?

| Beginning | Middle | End |
|---|---|---|
| • Today, we're going to ... | • Have a look at ... | • As you can see, ... |
| • Today, I'm going to ... | • You'll see that ... | • Any questions? |
| • We'll / I'll start by ... | • Next, let's look at ... | |

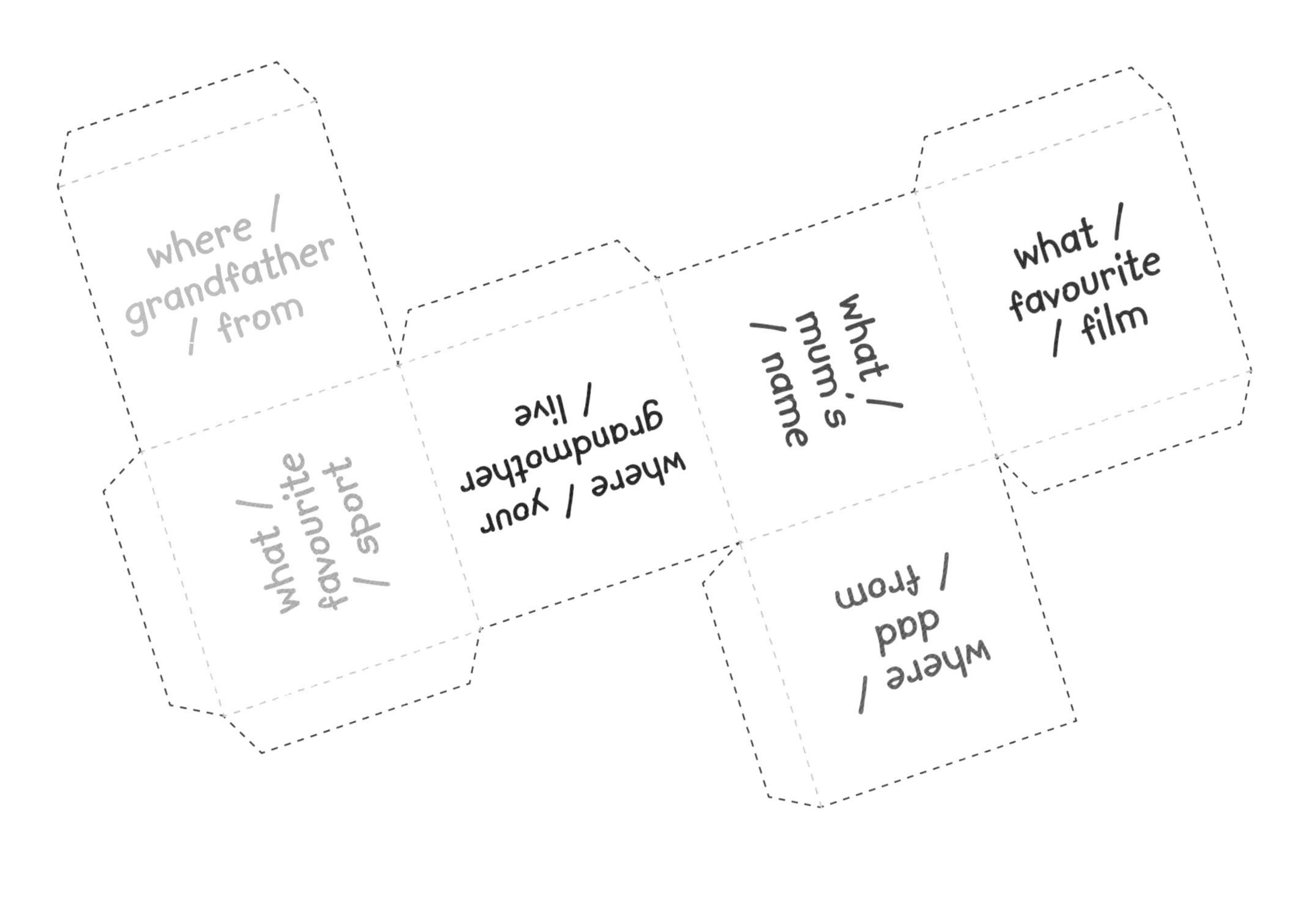


**Unit 2 Cutouts** Use with Activity 3 on page 47.

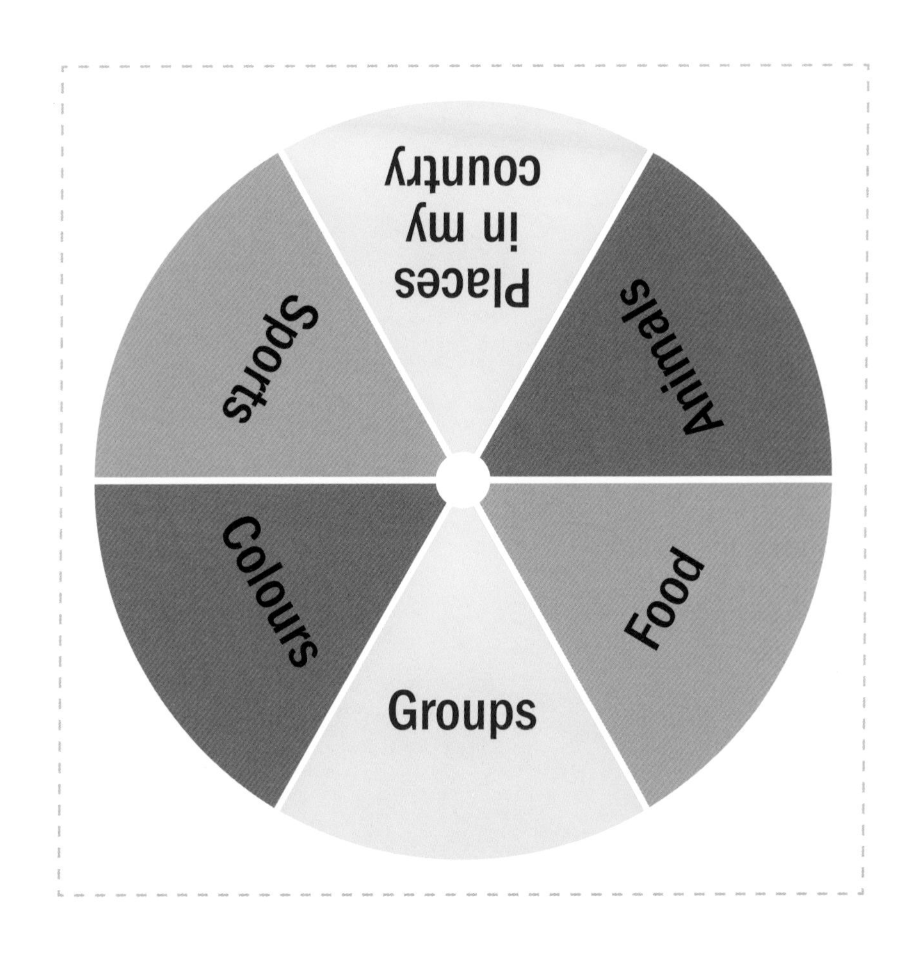

lunchbox
sandwiches
bowl
rice
bag
apples
cup
tea
board
bread
packet
sugar
plate
biscuits
box
potatoes
bottle
water
fridge
eggs

**Unit 2 Cutouts** Use with Activity 3 on page 54.

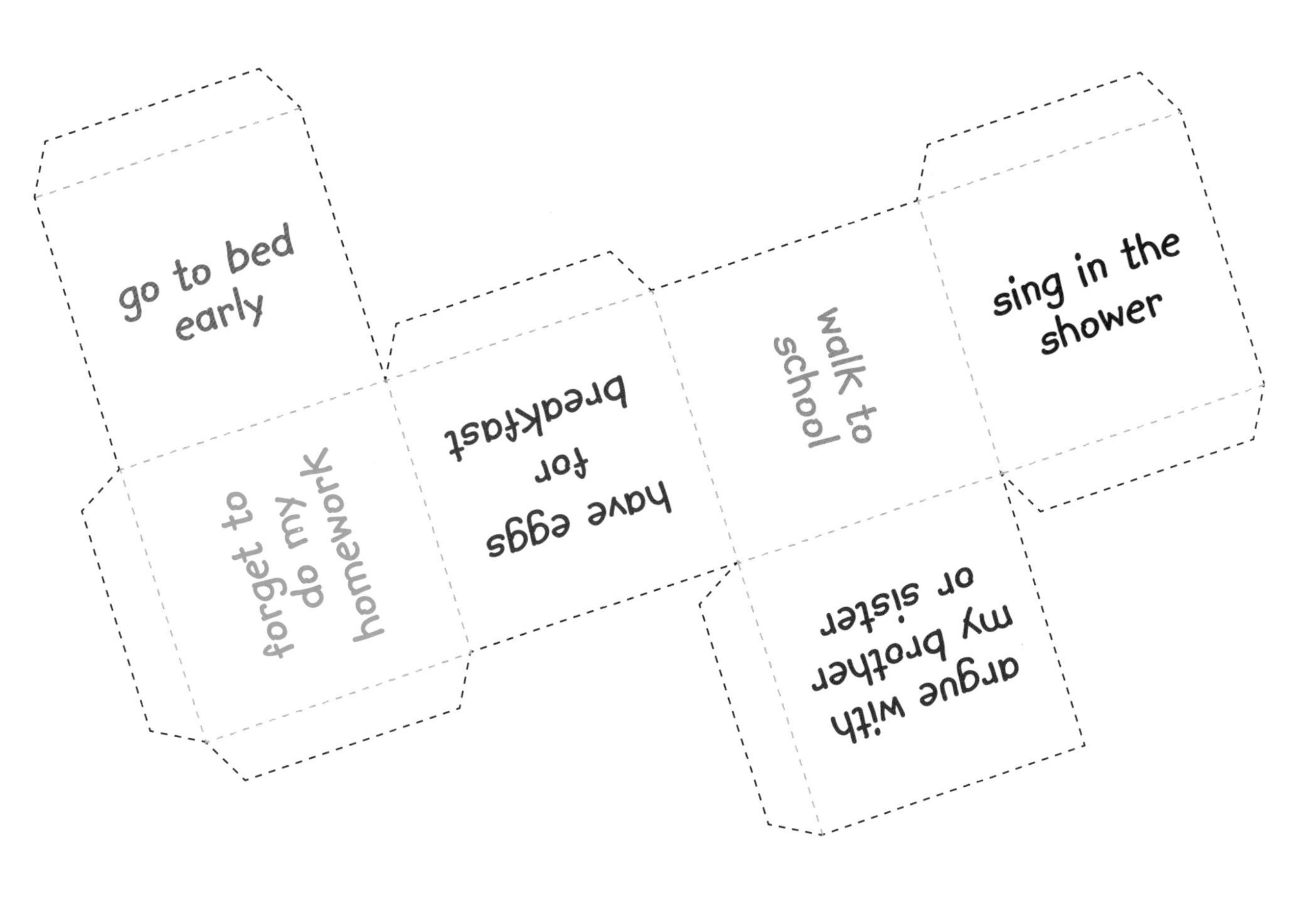


**Unit 6 Cutouts** Use with Activity 2 on page 122.

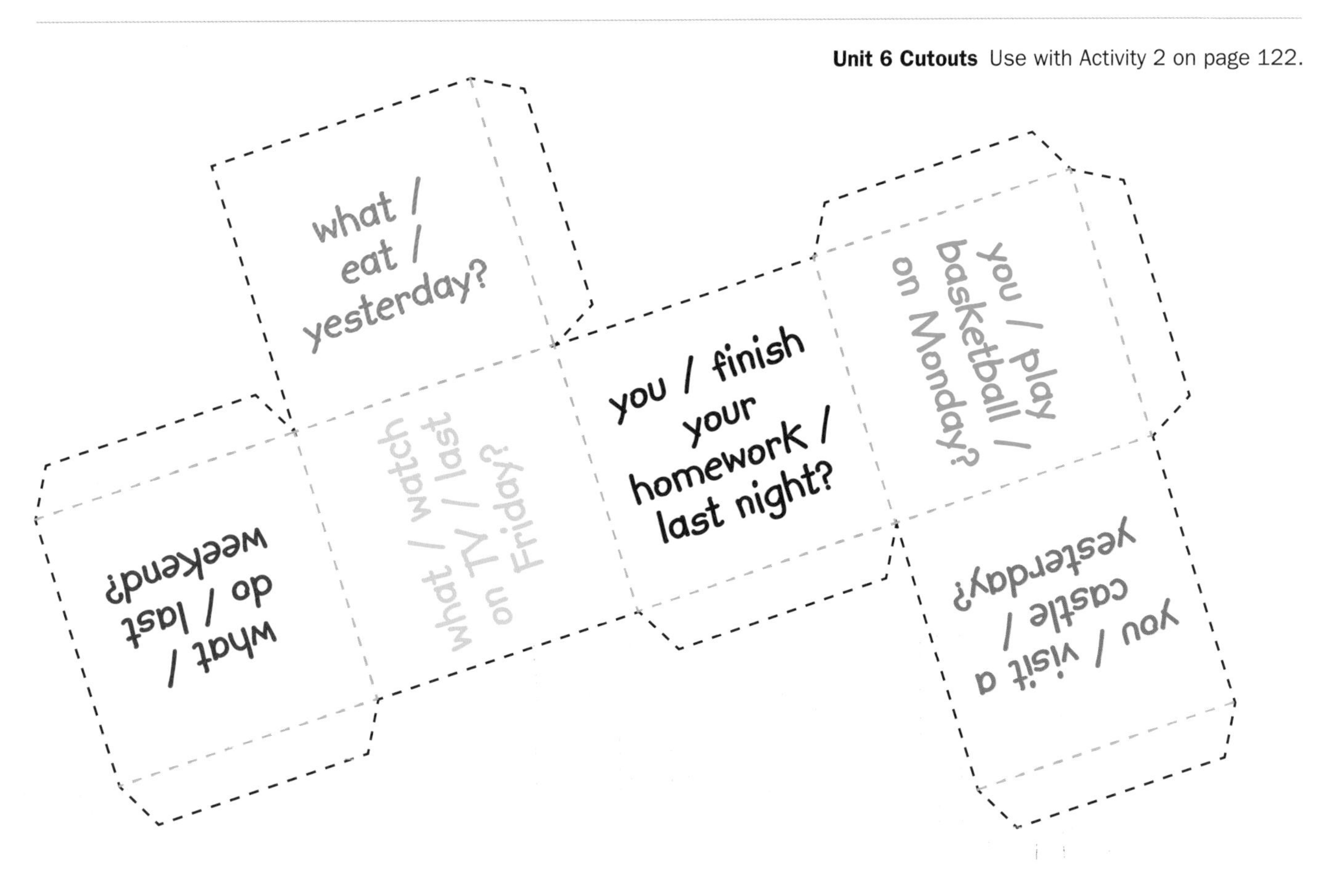

**The SuperClock** is a robot alarm clock. It jumps onto the floor and hides!

**Helidrone** flies around your home. It can take photos and videos.

**Tech-o-ball** looks like a ball, but you can control it with your phone and play a lot of games with it.

**Roboclean** cleans your floor.

**SpaceDroid** is an astronaut robot. It helps astronauts on the International Space Station.

**HandyReach** helps people who can't move their arms. It can pick up things.

**DogBot** is a robot dog. It can understand voice commands.

**Make it Basic** is a robot kit. You build the robot and you decide what it can do.

save water in the bathroom

keep our local river clean

protect local wildlife

eat healthy food at school

save water in the garden



I want to be a computer scientist.

I don't understand my maths homework.

I want to study engineering at university.

I want to buy a robot dog.

I want to build a robot.

I want to design computer games.

Foping Nature Reserve

Yala National Park

Ngamba Island Chimpanzee Sanctuary

Ranthambore National Park

Sepilok Orangutan Sanctuary

National Bison Range

**Foping Nature Reserve**

- Where: China
- Size: 350 square kilometres
- Number of pandas: 80–100
- Other animals: leopards, golden monkeys and black bears

**Yala National Park**

- Where: Sri Lanka
- Size: 979 square kilometres
- Number of elephants: 350
- Other animals: leopards, bears and buffalo

**Ngamba Island Chimpanzee Sanctuary**

- Where: Uganda
- Size: ½ square kilometre
- Number of chimpanzees: 49
- Other animals: wild birds and fish

**Ranthambore National Park**

- Where: India
- Size: 392 square kilometres
- Number of tigers: 22
- Other animals: hyenas, wild boar and leopards

**Sepilok Orangutan Sanctuary**

- Where: Borneo
- Size: 43 square kilometres
- Number of orangutans: 60–80
- Other animals: sun bears, gibbons and pygmy elephants

**National Bison Range**

- Where: USA
- Size: 74 square kilometres
- Number of bison: 350
- Other animals: bears, antelope and deer

start

rubbish on the grass / no rubbish on the grass

no birds in the park / birds in the park

plastic bags in the water / no plastic bags in the water

no people in the park / people in the park

**Great!** You help on a Park Clean-up Day. Throw the coin again.

no cycle paths / cycle paths

**Oh, no!** You throw a plastic bottle into the lake. **Go back to the start.**

an old car by the trees / no old car by the trees

finish

no benches for people / a lot of benches for people

dead fish in the lake / live fish in the lake

I prefer photos of buildings with people in them.

Some buildings are more important than other buildings.

Houses that all look the same are boring.

Museums are interesting places.

You can show your personality through your home.

Buildings from the past are more interesting than today's buildings.

I'm not interested in looking at buildings.

It's important to keep a record of our history.

**Unit 7 Cutouts** Use with Activity 3 on page 133.

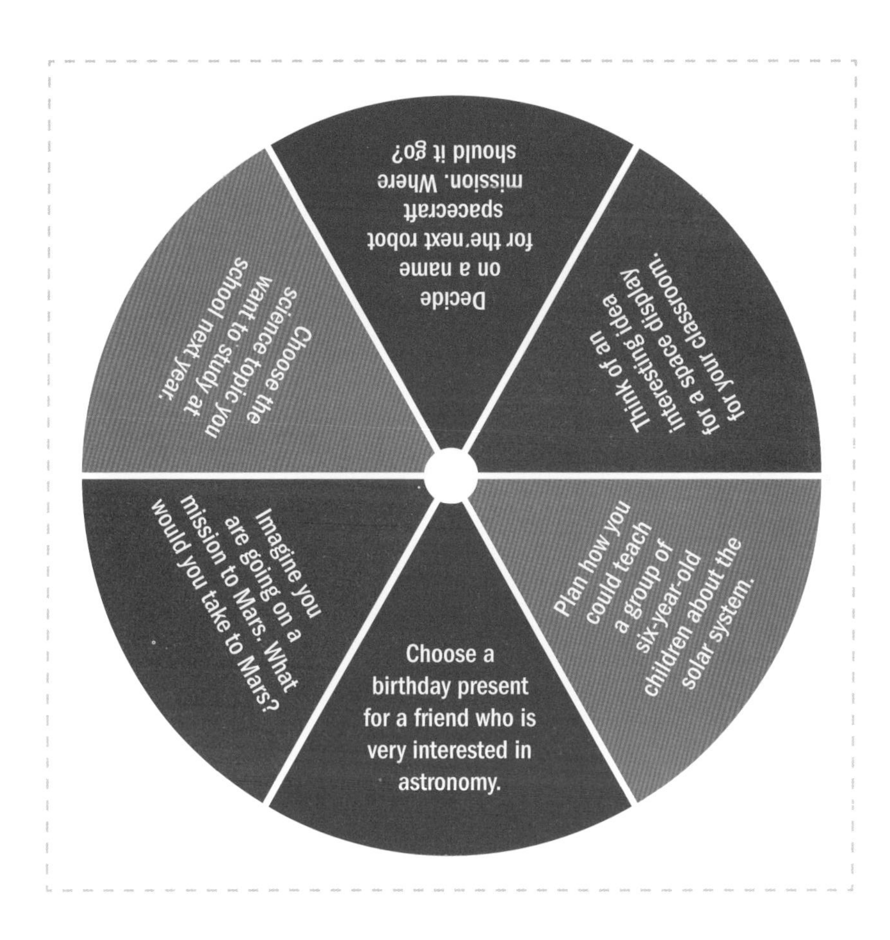


**Unit 8 Cutouts** Use with Activity 3 on page 156.

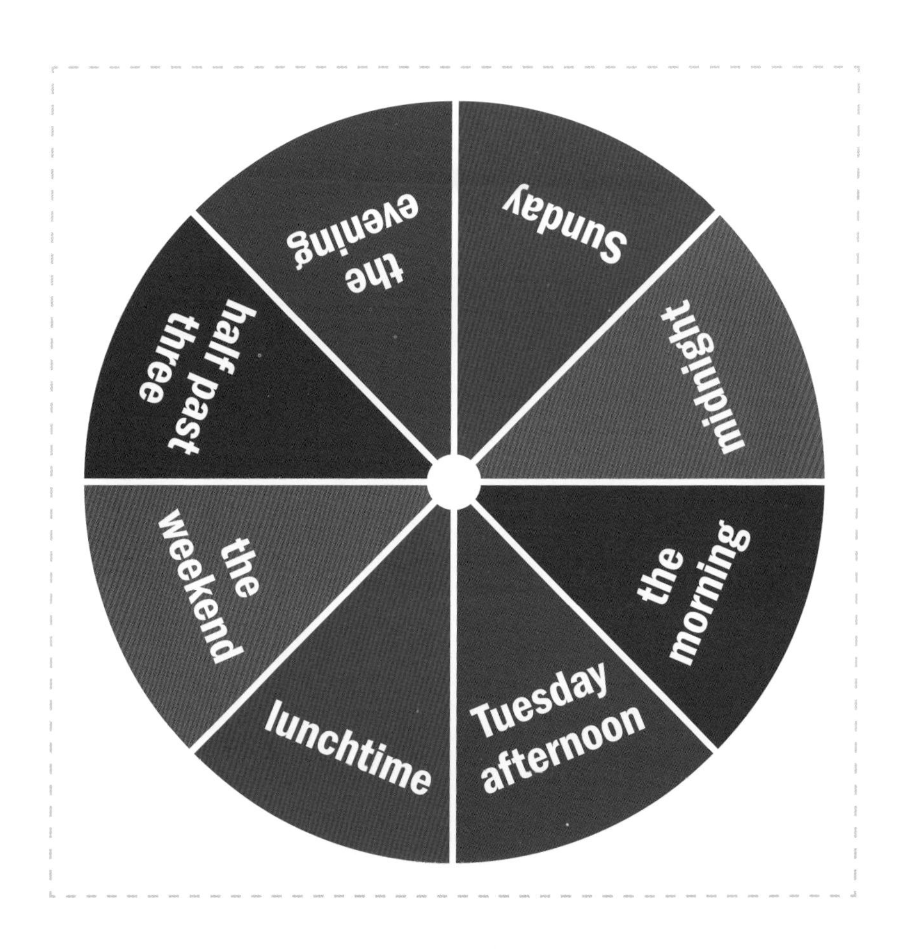

What / is / hot / planet / in our solar system?

Who / was / old / person / to travel to space?

What / is / big / planet / in our solar system?

What / is / famous / telescope / in space?

What / is / high / mountain / in the solar system?

Who / ran / fast / marathon / in space?

The ______ (hot) planet in our solar system is Venus. Its average temperature is 462°C (864°F).

Astronaut Tim Peake ran the ______ (fast) marathon in space on 24th April 2016. He ran the marathon in 3 hours, 35 minutes and 21 seconds on a running machine on the International Space Station.

Jupiter is the ______ (big) planet in our solar system. More than 1,300 Earths can fit inside Jupiter!

The Hubble telescope is the ______ (famous) telescope in space. It is a telescope and a camera, and it can see and photograph stars and planets millions of kilometres away.

The ______ (high) mountain in the solar system is Olympus Mons on the planet Mars. It is 24 km (15 mi) high.

The ______ (old) man in space was John Glenn. He travelled on the space shuttle Discovery in 1998, when he was 77 years old. John Glenn was also the first American to orbit Earth in 1962.

Prince Street

Lunenburg Academy

Visitor Information

Fisheries Museum of the Atlantic

Settlers' Memorial

Fishermen's Memorial

Kinley Drive

Supermarket